PRAISE FOR *EMOTIONAL DETOX*

"A warm, heartfelt, courageously powerful book with an extraordinary yet practical angle on how to free yourself from emotional wounds and trauma. I love this book! Study it and use it!"

—DR. SUSAN SHUMSKY, award-winning author of *Miracle Prayer*; *Instant Healing*; and thirteen other books

"*Emotional Detox* is a courageous story of true healing and unconditional love. It will wake you up and turn your views upside down while providing you with life-changing tools and insight. The C.L.E.A.N.S.E. formula was simple and easy to implement. Whether you are struggling emotionally or not, this book is a *must* read!"

—ELIZABETH HAMILTON–GUARINO, CEO of The Best Ever You Network and author of *Percolate* (Hay House)

"Sherianna Boyle—in her authentic, truthful, and soulful way—shares her most personal crisis in her newest book *Emotional Detox*. She skillfully guides you to find techniques and insights into healing your own emotional traumas. She shows you that by remaining grounded to your aligned state of being, you can generate a healing response to transform the event and yourself, and find opportunities to move past hurt to create something good, beautiful, and lasting. An indispensable tool for creating new habits and behaviors, accepting love and life, and knowing peace. Outstanding!"

—SHERYL GLICK, RMT (www.SherylGlick.com), host of *Healing from Within* and author of *Life Is No Coincidence* and *The Living Spirit*

PRAISE FOR *EMOTIONAL DETOX*

"In Sherianna's latest book *Emotional Detox*, she weaves personal trauma with detailed insight on how utilizing her own seven-step C.L.E.A.N.S.E. formula saved her life. We all tend to adjust our feelings for others instead of being our authentic selves. We have been taught reactivity instead of feeling what truly goes on within our emotions. Through her C.L.E.A.N.S.E. formula, we learn how to embrace our feelings and come to understand reactivity and why we overprocess our emotions. *Emotional Detox* is an excellent 'how-to' journey to living a full, joyful life."

—DEBORAH BEAUVAIS, Dreamvisions 7 Radio Network

"Sherianna brings invaluable experience, training, and research into the physical and psychological manifestations of our emotions and beyond. *Emotional Detox* outlines a mindful practice of tuning in to your emotions, honoring them, flushing out the negativity, and bringing us back to love. After reading it, I decided to make it a required text for the Kind Yoga Teacher Training Program. I want all of my future yoga instructors to know about the C.L.E.A.N.S.E."

—DIANE KOVANDA, MED, director of Kind Yoga (www.KindYoga.com), and meditation and mindfulness teacher trainer

"Sherianna Boyle bravely shares the story of her personal journey from crisis to wholeness, guiding the reader through her C.L.E.A.N.S.E. steps to their own emotional detoxification."

—MARY PETIET, author of *Minerva's Owls*

EMOTIONAL DETOX

7 STEPS TO
RELEASE TOXICITY AND
ENERGIZE JOY

SHERIANNA BOYLE, MED, CAGS

ADAMS MEDIA
NEW YORK LONDON TORONTO SYDNEY NEW DELHI

Adams Media
An Imprint of Simon & Schuster, Inc.
57 Littlefield Street
Avon, Massachusetts 02322

This Adams Media trade paperback edition January 2019

ADAMS MEDIA and colophon are trademarks of Simon & Schuster.

For information about special discounts for bulk purchases, please contact Simon & Schuster Special Sales at 1-866-506-1949 or business@simonandschuster.com.

The Simon & Schuster Speakers Bureau can bring authors to your live event. For more information or to book an event contact the Simon & Schuster Speakers Bureau at 1-866-248-3049 or visit our website at www.simonspeakers.com.

Interior design by Katrina Machado
Interior image © 123RF/Olga Grigorevykh

Manufactured in the United States of America

10 9 8 7 6

ISBN 978-1-5072-1000-0
ISBN 978-1-5072-0719-2 (ebook)

"Grace means that all of your mistakes now serve a purpose, instead of serving shame."

—Mike Rusch

To my love, Kiernan. Thank you for giving me permission to share our private journey.

To Joanne Audyatis, for being our tour guide through this process.

To our children, Megan, Mikayla, and Makenzie, who bring us great joy!

To mom Judy and father Larry, whom I love so much.

To Jason Peterson, thank you for all your support.

To everyone at Simon & Schuster—including Karen Cooper, Beth Gissinger, Brendan O'Neill, Alice Peck, Bethany Carland-Adams, Laura Daly, and Frank Rivera—who offered their time, creativity, and insight on this project. Thank you.

Dear Reader,

If you are drawn to this book, you have courage; if you have taken time to read it, you are bold. This means you instinctively know there is more to what is, has been, or may be happening inside you than is clear at first. You may be tired of digging, analyzing, or running away from your problems, or a part of you realizes if you could move past one or two obstacles, life would become more fulfilling. Deep inside you recognize that if you cleanse fear, insecurity, and doubt, you could create the life you desire and deserve. Within these pages, you'll discover how an emotional detox is a systematic and mindful way to purge those undigested emotions stuck inside you. Like a physical detox, an emotional detox allows you to remove unwanted impurities that prevent you from living a full and healthy life. An emotional detox will allow you to truly feel your emotions, teach you how to take care of your feelings, and provide a road map for living a happy, fulfilled life. I designed a seven-part C.L.E.A.N.S.E. method to walk you through an emotional detox, step by step:

- Clear
- Look Inward
- Emit
- Activate Joy
- Nourish
- Surrender
- Ease

Emotional detoxes are not about winning a battle; they are about transforming how you see yourself in the first place. Detoxes don't happen to you; they are *for* you, and when they are done with a sense of integrity and sincerity, they work *through* you.

Let's begin...

CONTENTS

INTRODUCTION

"I think I'm having an out-of-body experience."

"Tell me more," my therapist gently nudged.

"It feels like I'm watching my life, but I am not a part of it—kind of like a coma. I can see and hear everything, but I am not actually *in* my body."

She didn't bat an eye. "You're suffering from withdrawal."

What the heck? I didn't drink, smoke, or have any kind of addictions. "How can that be?"

"You're detoxing from your marriage—withdrawals aren't always about substances."

She was right. I needed to detox emotionally from my marriage crisis.

So what is an emotional detox? Well, it's an introspective process that helps you rewrite the negative stories, thoughts, and beliefs attached to your emotions. Like a food detox, an emotional detox leaves you feeling energized, clear, and fulfilled; it cleanses the pathway for new habits and behaviors, and lays the groundwork for connection, happiness, and love. It sounds like a big deal, and it is—but it's also a process that is easy to understand, provides meaningful progress with each step, and is a direct link to living an abundant life.

When I really thought about what an emotional detox is and does, I realized that my therapist was spot on; I was the perfect candidate for an emotional detox. My marriage was in flux after I found out about my husband's affair. I discovered the horrible truth two days after our eighteenth wedding anniversary as I stood in our kitchen breathing air fragrant from the dozen red roses he had sent. My husband had left his phone directly in front of the coffeepot—my first stop every morning. I looked at his messages, and that's when I discovered the secret life my husband had been living—*bam*! Never in a million years did I think this could or would happen to me…to *us*.

"Do you love her?" I asked him later.

"No, I love you." He was crying. "I've loved you the whole time, Sheri. I will be sorry for the rest of my life."

Even in the worst moments of my heartache and grief, something inside me knew this crisis was an opportunity. The process taught me that our heart's desire lies within the processing of raw emotions.

I had actually planned to write a book on emotional detox even before I found out about my husband's betrayal, but learning about the affair brought me physically and psychologically to my knees. An emotional detox was no longer something I could just teach others—I had no choice but to go through the process myself. In doing so, I studied firsthand how emotions can contribute to suffering and how working with them can bring relief and deep healing to a current situation as well as to the wounds of the past.

This was not the only time I've been in a place of disaster, shock, and fear. If you're reading this book, you may have dealt with some horrible news or may be making hard choices about what to do next in your life. That's why, while moving through my emotional detox, I began to research trauma. Before I knew it, my coaching clients were showing up at my office with one traumatic experience after another—breakups, lost jobs, addiction, and toxic relationships. My training as a psychologist helped me tap into science and research, while the healer part of me worked intuitively using mind-body techniques like meditation and yoga combined with the C.L.E.A.N.S.E. steps I share in this book. People who had been "stuck" in therapy for years were making amazing progress in just a few sessions. A woman who could not get out of a controlling marriage was now moving through the pain of her relationship with her father. A man who was addicted to heroin was learning how to feel his emotions rather than numb them. I was even getting referrals from therapists who suggested I see their clients a few times to help them move forward.

I was thrilled to contribute my part to these healing journeys, and as I did, my role as a C.L.E.A.N.S.E. coach developed. I began to see my situation in a brighter light...as my higher purpose. That's when I remembered a prayer I used to recite in the times before my husband's infidelity: "God, I am here. Tell me what would you have me do?"

I believe I have found the answer.

When we are faced with a challenging situation, we have two choices: hold onto our pain or heal it. What I have discovered is choosing to heal is no different from choosing joy. Our most natural state is joy. When we are in it, we feel light, effortless, smooth, confident, and free. What makes joy so powerful is its purity. It is an unfiltered state of unconditional love. Joy is abundantly and effortlessly alive, yet we let so many things—frustrations, mishaps, fears, anxieties, unhealthy relationships, and past experiences—taint it.

These emotions are not toxic, but the way in which we have conditioned ourselves to respond to them is—that's what I call *reactivity*. Here is the thing: we are born with emotions; reactivity is what we learn. Raw emotions are like nutrients, reactivity like toxins. No one comes into this world with denial, expectations, the urge to gossip, guilt, doubt, and insecurity—these are reactions reinforced by how we interpret and respond to our feelings.

No matter what you are going through or where you are in your life, joy is with you, I promise. Our spirits want to stay in sync with joy and avoid disconnection, but *joy can be stripped from life if we view life through a lens of fear.* Compromised emotions lower our standards. They create an environment in which we ignore, put up with, minimize, and in some cases, accept things that disrupt joy. Without joy we are likely to feel we are going through the busyness of our lives but never let our feet touch the ground long enough to stand in the truth of our emotions. Over time this can wreak havoc on our nervous systems and bodies—how they function and react to our daily experiences and emotions.

Here is the thing: no part of us knows joy better than the soul. If we feel disconnected, overworked, undervalued, or just plain stuck, we are ignoring our soul's ability to nourish us. Our feelings have a purpose. When they are sustaining and digested fully, like food they offer us tremendous energy. However, when our emotions are overprocessed, like chemical-laden foods, they linger in our bodies, create toxins and an inflammation of the mind, and diminish our well-being.

My hope is that by the end of your C.L.E.A.N.S.E., you will no longer dissect, diminish, devalue, or criticize what you are feeling. I hope you will fall in love with your emotions—not just those that make you happy but every single one of them as you clear away reactivity and become present to your emotional energy, courageously connected to your true purpose: *joy*.

PART I
TOXICITY

TOXICITY IS SOMETHING WE ALL ENCOUNTER AT ONE POINT OR ANOTHER AS WE JOURNEY THROUGH LIFE. WE HEAR ABOUT IT IN THE NEWS, OFTEN FROM AN ENVIRONMENTAL STANDPOINT. BUT WE ALL FACE ANOTHER TYPE OF TOXICITY AS WELL—EMOTIONAL. IN THIS PART, WE'LL LEARN MORE ABOUT THE INS AND OUTS OF AN EMOTIONAL DETOX AND HOW YOU CAN RID YOUR BODY OF HIGH LEVELS OF STRESS AND WORRY.

CHAPTER 1

WHAT IS AN EMOTIONAL DETOX?

"If you want to know your purpose, it is joy."

—Dr. Zoe Marae

If you are like me, you have grown accustomed to seeing a detox as a physical experience. A way to remove all the impurities swallowed, inhaled, injected, absorbed, and in some cases abused through daily living. Substances such as alcohol, drugs, caffeine, sugar, smoke, pesticides, parasites, and harsh chemicals may come to mind. Although physical improvements often occur, emotional detoxes have little to do with the physical and *everything* to do with you as a spiritual being. Emotional detoxes are a systematic and mindful practice for purifying undigested and overprocessed emotions, freeing us from the illusion that we are separate from love. They return us to our natural state of joy.

If you have heard yourself say, "I can't wait until this day (or week or month) is over," then, darling, you have opened the right book.

Like overprocessed and undigested foods that deplete energy (e.g., Tic Tac mints, which I happen to love), our emotions are so overprocessed by thinking that they become unnatural. We know when this happens—when our feelings are weird, foreign, or unappealing. Just as consuming sugar substitutes can trick our bodies into being hungrier, living in emotional reactivity tricks our bodies. We get a temporary and illusory feeling of being okay, but it doesn't last. This is because reactive emotions don't nourish us.

One might think the point of an emotional detox is to get rid of it all—hurt, pain, guilt, sadness, and stress—because when left unresolved these emotions can make us sick, but this is not the case. We need to properly process our emotions. Since our bodies are connected to our spirits, they don't benefit from all these toxins; what we thrive on is love. Learning how to process emotions through a detox will bring you closer to love.

To get rid of a feeling would be a reaction, like saying, "I am so done with him." Believe me, part of me would have given anything to get rid of my pain, to make my husband pay for his mistake, or to confront the stranger who contributed to his actions. Something inside of me—it may have been my higher self—told me that to react from anger would only do more harm. I believed there were great lessons to be learned if I trusted all would be cleared through an emotional detox. I was right.

Here is the thing: our emotions have value no matter how painful and upsetting they may be. Undermining, numbing, or pushing them away will only delay their benefits. Rather than a juice cleanse where you might flush out highly acidic foods and sugar, think of an emotional detox as a *reaction* cleanse, where you flush out high levels of stress, worry, and defensiveness.

Jeanie had been in therapy for years. When she came to me, she felt stuck, unmotivated, and depressed. She put a tremendous amount of pressure on herself and was often overwhelmed by what she perceived as her lack of progress past her symptoms of anxiety and physical pain. Things changed after I looked into her eyes and said, "Jeanie, you are reacting, therefore nothing you are telling me is real; it is all an illusion. Sure, it feels like crap, but the thing is you are not really feeling at all, you are reacting, and it is time to change this habit." I went on to say, "I know you feel rejected, unworthy, and frustrated. I have those feelings too; however, until you fully digest them (without reactivity), you are going to recycle these experiences. You can sit in your pain or make something good come out of it. The choice is yours."

The same was true for me, which was why I turned to an emotional detox. It wasn't until I was focused on things as they were that I was able to experience life in a new way. Whether you are moving through a traumatic experience, looking to release the past, or just want to create more positive experiences in your life, emotional detoxes will help.

SIGNS YOU COULD USE A DETOX

If you find yourself trying to fix everyone else's problems, feeling guilty for saying no, or becoming less engaged with the people around you, then you will receive help from a detox. If you take more time for others than you do for yourself or have experienced trauma, a detox is in order. If you are a thinker, dwell on life's problems, or are finding it hard to be in the present moment, an emotional detox is something to consider.

Here are some of the signs to look for:

- Being easily distracted
- Worrying about or being fearful of the future
- Losing or gaining weight
- Binge eating or eating too little
- Financial insecurity
- Relationship problems
- Lying to yourself or others
- Avoiding certain people or places
- Spending too much time alone
- Ignoring your gut feelings
- Feeling overwhelmed
- Considering or having an affair
- Drinking or doing drugs to escape the pressures in life
- Focusing (or being stuck) on the past more than the present
- Trouble speaking up for yourself
- Self-doubt or second-guessing your choices
- Feeling stuck or out of balance
- Being easily swayed by the opinions of others
- Comparing yourself to others or not feeling "good enough"
- Feeling like you work hard but nothing changes

There are also some physical symptoms, such as:

- Trouble sleeping
- Chronic tension

- Headaches
- Allergies
- Illness or pain
- Depression and anxiety

Other reasons to detox include:

- Looking to deepen your relationship with yourself and others
- Wanting to forgive, move on, or let go but being unsure how to do so
- Feeling stuck in the past
- Feeling lonely, too old, or unsure of your purpose
- Interested in learning how to be more present and mindful

WHAT YOU WILL LEARN

One of the greatest things you will learn from an emotional detox is how to digest your feelings both verbally and nonverbally. You will see how there is more to emotions than expressing them. Without awareness, talking about your feelings can be a form of reactivity.

If you have ever listened to others rant about their problems, you know what I mean. Let's say you listen to a mom at the playground vent about her lack of sleep. If you are a parent yourself, you'll probably relate to the feeling. Before you know it, you are in a discussion about sleep deprivation. Later you find yourself discussing this person's problems with someone else, because part of you feels guilty for not being able to help this mom out. That's a way of relating rather than digesting feelings.

Emotional detoxes teach the importance of digesting rather than reacting (thinking, fretting, fixing, remembering). Interestingly, as we digest our whole emotions, our ability to empathize with others without moving into reactivity improves. As a result, we can care and support others without clogging up our emotional flow, which can wreak havoc on our nervous system, creating things like anxiety and depression. This is an important skill to have in a world where each of us is so often exposed to trauma and tragedy in our daily lives and the world around us.

THINGS TO AVOID

Like plant-based diets or a regular exercise routine, emotional detoxes are a lifestyle. People on a diet have made a conscious decision to avoid eating certain foods. In a similar way, those who choose the pathway of an emotional detox have made a conscious decision to digest emotions, heal, and not consume reactivity. Most people I know who choose this lifestyle are clear this is a personal choice. They are mindful not to judge others. You may choose to digest, while others may continue to consume reactivity. That is their choice, and to truly be on the detox journey, we must respect each other's ways.

With that said, there are a few more things I recommend limiting or avoiding, particularly if you are going through a difficult time, such as experiencing a divorce, health issue, or high amounts of stress. The bottom line is you know yourself best. When approaching a painful anniversary, you might consider how the memory in your body might be triggered more than usual.

Because everyone heals at their own rate, I don't like to put timelines on emotional detoxes, but a good rule of thumb is it usually takes ninety days to change your brain and create a new habit, so during that time eliminate or limit:

- Alcohol or other mood-altering substances
- Nonprescription medications
- New or unnecessary situations like a job or move

- Time on the Internet or social media
- Sugary and high-salt foods and beverages
- Carbonated beverages (they interrupt digestion)
- Caffeine
- Eating late at night (this can disrupt sleep)
- Watching the news (read a newspaper instead so you can process the information instead of being assaulted by it)

Cutting back on these things will help you digest your raw emotions. So, let's talk about going raw.

GOING RAW

Think about a fresh carrot from the farmers' market versus a plastic bag of frozen carrots from the grocery store that have been processed, sometimes with chemicals—the frozen carrots will be far less nutritious and could even harm your system. Or consider eating a piece of fruit fresh off a tree—it will taste better, be easier to digest, and nourish you in a way a piece of apple-flavored candy can't.

It's the same with emotions. Going raw means digesting our pure emotions as they are, unfiltered by fears and anxieties. When they have been marinated in reactivity, we are more likely to resort to behaviors that overprocess them, such as thinking, analyzing, defending, and minimizing our strengths and abilities. Processing our emotions widens our lens, giving us the full scope of our attributes and possibilities, but *over*processing leaves us bombarded, frustrated, and hopeless.

Just as a physical detox increases our bodily energy, an emotional one increases our ability to connect and heal. Having energy is essential to creating the life we want—one of more meaningful relationships, acceptance, and love. Letting go of old ways and opening to new possibilities needs fuel, and without energy, you are likely to stay consumed, stuck, or hung up in old patterns. The good news is no trips to the market or pharmacy are necessary—a shift in awareness is all it takes. Here's how this will look:

GOING RAW (INCREASE ENERGY)	OVERPROCESSING EMOTIONS (DEPLETE ENERGY)
Feeling	Thinking
Noticing	Projecting
Observing	Reacting
Compassion	Criticism
Focused	Distracted
Allowing	Analyzing

One way that you can turn feeling into thinking is by choosing to follow your thoughts (brain) as opposed to observing your sensations (body). Like if you text someone and don't hear back, immediately you think that something has happened. You went from allowing your sensations to analyzing them. Analyzing burns off energy, while allowing creates it.

OPPORTUNITIES, NOT DETOURS

Our detox journey is about generating a healing inner space so that emotions become a form of nourishment, freedom, motivation, and guidance. You may not know which emotions you need to work on right now or if they are worth the effort; however, I want you to trust that *you* are worth it. Know an emotional detox will never hurt you. You can only gain from this experience, and anything that helps you will inevitably have a positive influence on others.

Emotional detoxes are opportunities, not detours. They are finding the best path, not overcomplicating things. They are about healing, not recovering. This is not to say there isn't a place or time for that; however, during an emotional detox seeing yourself "in recovery" may be a way to hold yourself back from opening to the possibilities, leading you to manage your emotions instead of *experiencing* them. This is because recovery has many interpretations—sometimes it can mean there is a chance for relapse while other times it means heading toward a cure. Healing, on the other hand, is about returning to wholeness. This is more in line with the detox mindset. It is important you understand that C.L.E.A.N.S.E. is by no means about "fixing" yourself.

People may overprocess their emotions because they see themselves as supporting their recovery. They hold themselves back from experiencing their feelings due to a past injury, emotional setback, or relapse. This could be as simple as eating a piece of cake after you have vowed to lay off the sweets or taking on an overwhelming task just as your life is becoming more balanced.

Recovery mindsets have a way of making us doubt our abilities and believe that whatever it is we are trying to avoid, stop, or change is going to happen again. This happens more often than you may think. Take a drive in busy traffic, spend some time talking to your mother about her problems, or work an extra long day, and you will see the shift. This is because we get hooked into a larger consciousness—a collection of people who feel the same way, people who feel overextended, disconnected, and rushed. If you are fully embracing your healing and have no fear about a setback or relapse, a recovery mindset may not interrupt the detox. However, if there is just an ounce of doubt, it may.

Here is the thing: your emotions don't fix you, they *are* you, and when you truly get this, you will begin to become your whole self.

EMBRACING THE UNKNOWN

What do you imagine the detox process will be like? What are some of the stories you have been telling yourself about your emotions? Do you believe processing them is going to be painful? Are you convinced that it is more than you can handle? If you think your emotions are something to avoid, then it makes sense you might avoid digesting them whole. If you have doused them in salt to hide the real flavor, to stay "strong," and to keep the status quo, slow down and take a moment to savor them in their pure form. Perhaps you have chosen to alter (or in some cases numb) sensations in another way, such as by drinking or binge-watching TV. I totally get it; when it came to experiencing emotions when my marriage was in trouble, I too put up barriers to "control" the painful and unknown, but be aware that blocking your emotions prevents you from digesting them.

As you start this journey, you may have no idea where you'll end up, and that is exactly how it is supposed to be. I want you to assume the unknown is exactly what you need right now. Think of it as an essential vitamin you have been low on. This may be challenging if you are used to being in control, even (and especially) if your life feels unmanageable. This is the way I had to treat the unknown during my detox—for the first time in my life, I felt I could not predict the outcome. Because we cannot control other people (we can only influence them), any sense of "control" I had was an illusion. To support the detox, I had to treat the unknown as an asset, a natural remedy to set me free from all the worry and angst I was carrying.

STAYING ON COURSE

Once you learn about your emotions, how they work, and what interferes with your ability to process them, you will begin to make subtle changes in the way you react to day-to-day experiences. You will learn how strong emotions may be re-exposing you to trauma when you dwell on the past and let your imagination run wild. Rather than waiting until things feel out of control and yelling, avoiding, stressing out, or making rash decisions, the C.L.E.A.N.S.E. steps will show you how to process the emotions that are underdeveloped or hardened within your brain and body.

This will take faith, which is where embracing the unknown comes into play. I am not exaggerating when I say this process brings you closer to your higher power. Before finding out about the affair, I remember reciting the mantra, "Jesus, let nothing come between You and me." With that said, I must admit, once I learned about the infidelity, I did go through a day or two of being upset with the Lord. I remember my husband sitting next to me as I sobbed into my hands and said, "All those prayers...and this is what happens?" I want you to know the Divine works in mysterious ways, and the results will come if you stick with the program. Trust that you are exactly where you are supposed to be, and for goodness sake, let go of any idea that your pain is your fault.

When it comes to embracing the unknown, we trip ourselves up. We look for—and in some cases attach to—evidence. We may look for cues that another person has changed, which pours doubt into the process of an emotional detox. Doubt is a reaction, not an emotion. I will talk about this when we explore how detoxes get sabotaged, but for now remember doubt is no different than going on a diet and then binging on sugar. If self-doubt surfaces, know it is because you are reacting rather than experiencing your emotions. When this occurs (and it will!), pause, take a breath, and trust that your awareness and the C.L.E.A.N.S.E. steps will lead you back to wholeness.

BEING CHALLENGED

People are going to challenge you on your detox. They are going to expect (and in some cases demand) that you see your emotions and your past from a perspective of right or wrong, good or bad. They are going to resort to their old rules, behaviors, patterns, judgments, and conditions. They are going to view everything as a timeline— past, present, and future. They might say things like, *Stay strong. Let go. Try harder. Do it my way. Fight back. Be careful.* They are going to project and force their opinions on you and in some cases question your judgment. Without awareness you may feel poked, prodded, pressured, and swayed by others to abandon the detox process.

This is because right now your life is scaring the hell out of them. You may even trigger their own unresolved emotions and trauma. Why? Because most often people don't plan on needing an emotional detox. It happens without warning: a divorce, diagnosis, relapse, freak accident, death, job loss, and, for me, an affair. This is not to say you cannot consciously choose to have an emotional detox. Now that I have seen the benefits in myself and others, I highly recommend making it a regular part of your self-care routine. For example, think about a physical detox, in which you might avoid high-sugar foods and preservatives because your intention is to lose weight and feel more fit, but you end up finding other things such as seasonal allergies or skin conditions have healed as well. Emotional detoxes work in the same way, as we are likely to cleanse rage and fear and find ourselves gaining self-confidence, clarity, and strength.

It might seem like an emotional detox would be more painful than stewing in the familiar reactive emotion; however, this is not necessarily the case. Emotional detoxes are emotional detours—they take us away from what is "normal" and into the unfamiliar. As this occurs, we get to see how strong we are, how deeply and unconditionally we can love, what trust is about, and how processed emotions lead to joy.

Most of all, emotional detoxes are about surrendering. They encourage us to release old ways of being—all the trying, waiting, pleasing, and avoiding—and instead wake up to what is real. We are spiritual beings having a transformational experience. You can choose to resort to old ways of harboring and overfocusing your emotions or experience them wholly as they are. Digesting whole emotions is a way to live more simply, ditch the drama, thrive in any situation, and reconnect to your organic self.

CLEANSING TIP: SALT SOAK

If you are sensitive to negativity or have been physically or emotionally under stress, consider soaking for ten minutes or more in a saltwater bath. If you don't have a bathtub, consider taking a footbath. You can use sea salt or Epsom salt. Saltwater naturally removes what no longer serves you, creating space for what does. Think about how purified you feel after a dip in the ocean. The bath will relax your body, allowing your emotions to move freely. The salt will pull out any mental and emotional stress you have absorbed. Be sure to close your eyes and take some deep breaths while soaking.

CHAPTER 2

BENEFITS OF AN EMOTIONAL DETOX

"Therefore, if anyone is in Christ, he is a
new creation; the old has gone, the new has come."

—2 Corinthians 5:17

Learning to process our emotions can be like gaining superpowers. Just as you might feel energized from a fruit smoothie loaded with vitamin C and antioxidants, emotional detoxes also build your immune system, lifting vitality and generating a more youthful attitude and appearance. I can't tell you how often I have watched the strain in people's faces and bodies diminish as they allowed themselves to fully digest their emotions. This allows them to relax, to become more flexible and open to seeing things in a new way. A shift in perception is nothing short of a miracle—it's the possibility of believing in something so strongly you could make it happen.

Emotional detoxes give us the means to metabolize our feelings. Living with this newfound dynamism can lead to improved health, relationships, and financial flow; a balanced body; and connection to your higher purpose. The C.L.E.A.N.S.E. steps taught me how to let go, to trust my feelings, and to quit weathering the storms—now I embrace them, and by doing so I process emotions instead of swallowing them whole. Each time I go through the steps, I can trust that I am on the path, instead of hoping that I'll find it.

In this chapter, you will learn how emotional detoxes supercharge your desires, the tremendous benefits of raising your energy, how to truly let go, how the C.L.E.A.N.S.E. formula allows you an opportunity to get your needs met, why diets don't work, how emotional detoxes promote youthfulness and core strength, and what happens when things don't get detoxed.

SUPERCHARGED MANIFESTING!

I never set out to create a formula for manifesting. It happened on its own through my dedication to the C.L.E.A.N.S.E. steps. During the development of the formula, I was careful to integrate the spiritual law of attraction—the idea that what we focus on expands. This is why the C.L.E.A.N.S.E. steps never encourage you to focus on what is wrong with your life. Instead the formula captures the energy you will be using to manifest your desires through the processing of your emotions.

Initially the formula was designed to help me (and eventually my clients), and it worked! Repeatedly I saw traumas and childhood wounds heal and dissolve. The triggers eventually diminished, and if they returned, the formula extinguished their charge. It was as if practicing the steps daily supported the flow of energy it created. I even practiced the C.L.E.A.N.S.E. steps on the days I felt grounded and calm. Some days it almost felt haphazard, but it was never about doing or being perfect.

Then, something cool happened…

Things started manifesting. Seeds I had planted years ago were beginning to grow and bloom. Book sales increased, and new opportunities came my way. The best part is, things didn't just improve for me but also for my family. My husband and children grew and thrived in ways previously unimaginable. I saw tremendous growth in my clients as well, as the C.L.E.A.N.S.E. formula gave them insights and hope.

Here is the thing: seeds cannot be nourished with toxic water. You must dissolve reactivity first and embrace your whole emotions. The purity of these emotions feeds your dreams. Manifesting is a process that begins with healing. This includes some of your most tender relationships. It then evolves into surrender and slowly emerges into connection and ease. The C.L.E.A.N.S.E. formula is the answer.

GAINING FLOW

Once you develop energy from the processing of your emotions, life will flow more easily. As a result, you won't have to exhaust your body or mind with all that thinking and stressing out. Instead you begin to get to know yourself as a creator, and any type of creation means an increase of energy. We must become a vibrational match for what it is we choose to create. If you want more money, then you must become a vibrational match for being in flow. Money can either be an exchange of goods and services (flow) or a distraction. If it is a distraction, meaning you are consumed with having, keeping, or losing it, then you are probably in reactivity. There is a difference between being careful and consumed: *careful* means paying attention to what is happening; *consumed* means focusing on preventing what *might* happen.

Emotional detoxes increase your energy through the downloading and processing of emotions in the absence of reactivity. This means that when we can create space between our emotions and reactions, we can absorb the energy our emotions offer. You will know your energy is increased because you will be more tolerant, patient, and open to new ways of responding, such as taking deep breaths before starting a conversation. These changes happen because emotional detoxes increase self-awareness. The more aware we are, the greater our energy. If you want to be abundant, you must first feel abundant; you cannot become something you don't feel inside. The processing of raw emotions is what allows us to move from doing to becoming.

> After the affair, my husband and I found a wonderful Imago therapist who taught us how we could heal the childhood wounds that were surfacing. Imago therapy is a style of therapy that focuses on growth and healing. Although I have so much respect for Harville Hendrix (the creator of Imago) and am grateful for the process, inside I knew that I needed to pair the work with my own form of self-nourishment—the C.L.E.A.N.S.E. steps.

So many of us have grown accustomed to receiving energy from sources outside ourselves like food, water, caffeine, sex, relationships, sugar, compliments, status, approval, money, and community. However, this energy doesn't last—we return for more. Getting a raise for a job well done can boost your emotional outlook; however, unconscious, overprocessed emotions can eventually seep through, leaving you feeling frustrated, down, and wanting more.

I once had a client who moved out of his apartment because he was having a difficult time with his roommate. Things seemed to get better until he started disliking his new living situation. Once again, he had a difficult time connecting with his neighbors and feeling at ease in his own home. These were indications that the emotions he felt that led to the first move were never digested. I suggested before he make another decision he work through the C.L.E.A.N.S.E. steps because they offer a long-term solution to not only gaining but *sustaining* energy levels. They gave him the means to process what was triggering him, which in his case was unresolved anger.

As you learn to gain energy by processing your emotions, you will find yourself living a life on stable ground, meaning you will become more resilient, alert, self-assured, and inspired by how your emotions (when processed) hold everything you need to create the life you want.

SIMPLICITY

Emotional detoxes keep things simple. Rather than getting into all the labels, categories, and stories you have told yourself about what you are feeling, the C.L.E.A.N.S.E. steps encourage you to name your emotions as either *fear* or *love*. We've all seen what can happen when we get tangled in the story of our emotions, like when we call ourselves anxious or create stories to substantiate our negativity, such as being overworked and undervalued. While being overworked might be the case, often the true source behind the negativity is the amount of energy it takes to hold back what you are feeling. At times like this it can be difficult to recognize the difference between the heart and mind. Just as eating too fast can lead to unexpected bloating, hiccups, and discomfort, rushing through emotions—by thinking and talking instead of feeling—can do much of the same. These triggers without consciousness can lead us down a pathway of emotional reactivity. As a result, our bodies no longer feel safe, and rather than process our emotions they protect us from them.

Seeing things as either a state of love or fear takes all the guesswork away. We don't have to figure things out, analyze, or worry we are doing it wrong. If you feel open, neutral (less reactive, charged), and more present in your body, then you are coming from love, and with love comes joy. This is the state that puts a smile on your face even if your day has been lousy. Anything else falls in the realm of fear, especially when we feel pain or agony.

During our healing journey after the affair, my husband requested that it be referred to as "the fall" because it was his fall as a man from grace. This helped me pay attention and tune in to how certain words such as *affair* can interrupt healing. While terms such as *affair*, *breakup*, *addiction*, and *anxiety* can be useful in naming a problem, labels such as these can be a way to manage fear—as if by giving it a label, we've worked through it. This is something I share with the anxiety groups I lead. I tell people that the term *anxiety* got them in the door, but identifying as anxious, depressed, or crazy has no purpose in the healing process.

SWEET SURRENDER

Emotional detoxes teach the difference between letting go and surrender. Surrender is one of our most natural states; letting go is not. When we focus on letting go, in many ways we are putting our attention on what it is we are holding onto (fear, hurt, pain). We want to learn to let it flow because there lies the process of surrender. Surrender means we are allowing what is coming up to be healed. We are focused on the release rather than the trigger. You will know the difference by how you feel in your body.

LETTING GO	SURRENDER
Increases anxiety	Promotes calming
Focuses on releasing the past	Tunes in to the present moment
Takes energy	Cultivates energy
Manages emotions	Processes emotions
Pushes away	Allows
Unnatural	Natural

I found when I focused on letting go, this interrupted (rather than supported) the emotional detox because it made me focus on the affair. I also believe telling someone to let go of a horrific experience without awareness can come across as insensitive or unrealistic. If you live in a war zone, it's not prudent to "let go" of vigilance. Surrender, on the other hand, carries compassion. I'll go into this further when I talk about how detoxes get sabotaged, but for now know that if you have been struggling with moving on and letting go, it is your soul guiding you to your most natural state of surrender.

As you progress through the emotional detox, not only will you experience how to surrender but you will also come to recognize how some of the things you may have been taught about letting go don't work. Suggestions such as *just let it go, move on, ignore them, walk away, don't pay attention*, or *don't let it bother you* may redirect your attention; however, they don't teach you how to process the emotions. Practicing the steps will.

Months after the affair, I got dressed up to go out to dinner with my husband. He walked into the room looking and smelling so good, and I burst into tears. He looked at me and said, "Let's not let it get in the way and go out and have good time, okay?" We did have a great time, but that was because the C.L.E.A.N.S.E. steps helped me choose to surrender to the healing process.

SOUL BLISS

As you process your emotions, you will begin to experience what I call *soul bliss*. Think of soul bliss as coming home after a long journey. Only rather than your home being a physical place, it is your most natural state. When emotions become toxic with reactivity, we lose a sense of self, and as a result we feel a little lost, lost from the authenticity of who we are. Consequently, we might do and say things that are completely out of alignment with our true feelings. Emotional detoxes have a way of bringing us back, connecting us to our core values and intentions.

As human beings we tend to define each other by age, gender, race, occupation, or socioeconomic position; however, that is not how our souls recognize us. The soul defines us through the energy of our emotions. Our spirit doesn't spot us by our things, body, or even accomplishments, but instead it relates to our energetic frequency. When we choose to shut down, close off, or ignore emotions, we are separating ourselves from our spirit.

What I didn't expect when I did first my emotional detox was how, the more I was able to *be me*, the better things were. To be myself fully, I had to process (rather than think about) my emotions. During my husband's affair, there were times I sensed something was off, but I convinced myself he was stressed about work and took it as a sign that I needed to work harder and do more for the kids so things could return to being good. However, there was a part of me that was convinced this was as good as it was going to get, and as a result I ignored my gut feelings. Rather than become curious about his whereabouts, I focused on other things like writing, the kids, and clients because a part of me was afraid of what I might discover.

Here's the thing: you cannot be defensive and blissful at the same time. If you are keeping your guard up, you are denying the bliss your soul can bring. It is through this connection you will be able to truly turn on your manifesting powers, and as this occurs you will find life flows with more joy, ease, and love.

Sam and Jane came to see me as a couple. I had been counseling Sam privately, and he wanted to introduce Jane to the C.L.E.A.N.S.E. formula. When it came to Step 2—Look Inward— Jane was surprised to see all the tension surfacing in her body as she sat in the room with Sam. What we learned in that session was how Sam could come on a little strong with his feelings. Jane needed more time and space to process what he was saying. As he provided her with this space (through pausing and breathing), Jane's defenses (tension) started to release, and she was surprised to see how the space was filled with warmth and comfort. In a matter of moments, she went from defensiveness to bliss.

This is what it is like to be in soul bliss. Things just work out naturally without a lot of effort and strain.

GETTING YOUR NEEDS MET

Emotional detoxes are the pathways to learning how to get your needs met. I don't know about you, but there have been plenty of times I have felt myself biting my tongue, holding back from expressing my true thoughts, and placing the needs of others ahead of mine. Because my husband was making more money than I was, I convinced myself that he deserved more free time, that it was my duty to make up for bringing in less. This shifted for me as I realized it was a reaction to what I was controlling (i.e., emotions). The affair helped me realize that so much of my worth was dependent on the way my husband viewed me. Rather than experiencing my feelings, I was creating stories about them. My commitment to the formula was a way for me to build my self-esteem.

The stories we choose to tell ourselves about why we do and say the things we do are often unhealthy ways of covering up our needs. As you begin to incorporate the C.L.E.A.N.S.E. steps into your life, you will learn there is absolutely nothing wrong with having needs and asking for more. The steps will not only give you the courage to ask for what you want but also to accept support, love, and kindness when it is offered.

GROWING LIGHTER (WHY DIETS DON'T WORK)

Most diets don't work because they focus on loss. Diets encourage you to slim down, shed pounds, and banish the old you. This mindset couldn't be further from what your soul came here to do, which is why I call the C.L.E.A.N.S.E. process an emotional *detox*, not an emotional *diet*. Your soul wants you to be you. The real you doesn't stay the same; it expands, grows, and learns daily. To evolve in mind, body, and spirit, your soul needs to be nourished well, just like your body. Ideally foods that are closest to their most natural state are best, and the same goes for emotions. If you are turned off by fresh vegetables, it is because you have conditioned yourself to want processed food and quick fixes. When it comes to soul development there are no quick fixes; growth comes from connection, respect, and creativity. Foods high in nutrition have a life force (e.g., greens), while ones that are overprocessed (just like our emotions) don't.

Before the detox, I would inhale cheese—loved it. My stomach would grunt and groan after, yet I would just ignore it. I allowed my taste buds to override my bodily signals. Incorporating the C.L.E.A.N.S.E. steps taught me how to slow down, chew more slowly, and feel what it is like to digest my food. I saw how this related to my overprocessed feeling of insecurity about my marriage. I saw how this related to my overprocessed feeling of fear.

Food and emotions are similar. Swallow them (without awareness) and you find yourself feeling sluggish and bloated. Emotional detoxes teach you how to ditch the attachment to losing weight and instead focus on increasing energy through natural foods, exercise, and the digestion of your raw emotions.

Emotional detoxes help us sustain a healthy weight. Because the C.L.E.A.N.S.E. formula is based on self-awareness, it is a great help in creating a positive relationship with food, especially if you are someone who reacts to emotions by mindless eating or calorie counting. If that's you, then you may be ingesting more toxins than you know. At first you may feel better, fuller, slimmer, or more in control; however, over time these methods weaken your connection to your emotions because they are a reaction to what you are feeling. Reactions provide the foundation for disconnection. Nothing is more toxic than this disconnection. Emotional detoxes raise awareness, and as this occurs we get to make choices that are more in line with our visions and goals.

HEALING YOUR BODY

According to researcher, pioneer of mind-body science, and professor Candace B. Pert, PhD, "The body is the unconscious mind! Repressed trauma caused by overwhelming emotion can be stored in a body part, thereafter affecting our ability to feel that part or even move it." When teaching yoga, I have seen many people with an inability to move a certain part of their body—frozen shoulders, extremely tight hips—with no real "cause." Although the yoga postures and movements seem to help, it isn't until these people start the C.L.E.A.N.S.E. formula that I begin to see a change (for the better) in their bodies.

One of the benefits of the C.L.E.A.N.S.E. formula is it can easily be integrated into activities like yoga, groups like Al-Anon, or other types of support communities, which can incorporate the steps to shift participants into healing mode so that everyone can walk away feeling lighter and stronger and with less reactivity.

YOUTHFUL SKIN

Weeks after finding out about the affair, I woke up one morning, looked in the mirror, and did not recognize myself. I looked like I had aged twenty years. The skin on my face was drained from limited blood supply, leaving me with harsh lines and sagging skin. I remember taking an ice pack and lying down on the couch in an attempt to get the blood flowing back into my face. What I learned that day was the impact overprocessing your emotions can have on your skin and face. Emotional detoxes teach how to reduce tension, and as this occurs your skin no longer must hold onto the heaviness of your overprocessed emotions.

The mind-skin connection is nothing new. The skin is the largest organ in the body and happens to be the first thing we see when we look at ourselves in the mirror. It is no surprise that when we are stuffed with anger, riddled with guilt, or exhausted by life stressors, that those around us can recognize our state in our face and body. Again, our emotions are not bad—it is our reaction to them that holds them in place, affecting the elasticity of tissue and skin, forcing our muscles and organs to carry their weight. Emotional detoxes rid the body of this burden, and as a result we feel lighter, more flexible, and youthful.

If you want to learn more about the mind-body-skin connection, check out Kate Somerville's article "The Emotional Connection to Beautiful Skin" on Oprah.com, which explores how unresolved emotions can cause skin flare-ups such as acne, eczema, and wrinkles.

CORE STRENGTH

I am going to put myself out on a limb here and say it is difficult to process emotions without core strength. The reason being, your core is connected to your spine, which is the energetic highway of emotions. Candace B. Pert confirmed this saying, "Neuropeptides [can] be found not only in the rows of nerve ganglia on either side of the spine, but in the end organs themselves." She explains that neuropeptides are "the biochemical basis of emotion." To have a healthy spine, you must have a strong, healthy, balanced core. So, with that said, one of the amazing benefits of an emotional detox is strengthening those abs!

Here is the thing: the C.L.E.A.N.S.E. steps will teach you how to breathe properly, align your spine, and develop your posture. Healthy posture—whether you are standing or sitting—like digesting food, promotes healthy digestion of emotions. The steps mimic a similar technique to pull your abs in (contraction) and release them. This holding and squeezing action will strengthen your core (among other things). The stronger you feel in your core, the less you will be overwhelmed by your emotions.

WHEN THINGS DON'T GET DETOXED

According to author and healer Deepak Chopra, "If we don't deal with pain when it occurs, it will resurface as compounded emotional toxicity later on—showing up as insomnia, hostility, and anger, or fear and anxiety. As a further complication, if you don't know how to deal with feelings of anger and fear, you're likely to turn them inward at yourself, believing, 'It's all my fault.' That guilt depletes our physical, emotional, and spiritual energy until any initiative or movement feels impossible. We feel exhausted and paralyzed, leading to depression."

As I was putting together the C.L.E.A.N.S.E. steps, I had a client who was stuck in unemployment. Although he wanted to get a job, be independent, and quite frankly get everyone off his back, he couldn't get out of his own way. The more people harped on him to get a job, the less motivated he became. The detox revealed there was a part of him stuck in waiting—waiting for love. Not just romantic love but love that appeared lost or injured earlier in life. So many of the behaviors I come across are due to an internal energetic energy of wounded love. It would be through the detox that he would begin to inhale and receive the breath that would allow him to shake the hurt and get on with his life.

Often, wounded love, like the absence of a parent or cruelty from a sibling, can be the true source behind a lack of motivation, withdrawal, or procrastination. Clients who experience this have given me tremendous hope, and insight into the power of mind-body techniques.

When things do not get detoxed, your body is forced to escalate. It does this by turning up the volume and intensity of your symptoms. It is the only way it can truly be seen or heard. In fact, inflammation can mean that you're in need of an emotional detox. It can be physical inflammation, such as a sore throat (holding back your true feelings), skin rashes (irritability), and headaches (self-criticism and fear). Or you may have emotional symptoms, such as an excessive amount of self-doubt, fear, and poor self-esteem. Wellness pioneer Louise Hay wrote many books that are a great resource if you want to know more about the emotional causes of your symptoms. The good news is if you are suffering from any kind of illness, emotional detoxes are a wonderful addition to medical or nonmedical forms of treatment. You may even find your medical program changes (e.g., chiropractic adjustments and other doctor visits) once some of the emotions are detoxed.

CLEANSING TIP: HYDRATE

According to the US National Library of Medicine, part of the National Institutes of Health, increasing water intake results in a significant improvement of mood and physiological sensations. Sensations are how we experience emotional movement, how we know we are detoxing reactivity and digesting wholeness. Be sure to increase your water intake (eight glasses per day) while moving through this process.

CHAPTER 3

WHAT ARE YOU DETOXING?

*"Transformation is often more about
unlearning than learning."*

—Richard Rohr

Everything that is happening outside of you is a reflection of what is happening inside of you, even if you are choosing not to notice it. Boy, did I learn this the hard way! During the affair, I had done a good job convincing myself that my life was on the right track. I had just published *Choosing Love* and was working on my sixth book, *Mantras Made Easy*. In my mind, I was living my dream, being able to make a living helping others and doing the things I love. In many ways things were going quite well. However, what I chose not to pay attention to was the uneasiness I felt around my husband and how the tension in my home seemed to be increasing. I chalked it up to living with teenagers, being in a long-term marriage, and well...maybe that was what getting older was all about. *I was wrong.*

What I didn't know then is uneasiness and tension are signs of resistance, triggered trauma, absorbed emotions, and old behavioral patterns. These would end up being some of the things I needed to detox and that you might as well. Each of these concepts is described in the following pages of this chapter.

RESISTANCE

Think of resistance as a dam that prevents the flow of water, only instead of water it is preventing the flow (the processing of) emotions. It is not the fear, nervousness, and sadness that grow toxic but the unconscious ways we choose to resist experiencing them. The target of the C.L.E.A.N.S.E. detox is resistance. When we resist, we lose energy. One of the ways this can happen is through blame. When we blame our feelings or situation on someone or something, we project rather than digest the feelings. Think of blame (or any resistance) like vomit. It just doesn't sit well in the body. Here is the thing, sweetie, it is not the emotion that is causing your drain but the resistance to digesting it fully.

Overprocessing your emotions originates in resistance. It is this overprocessing that leads to trauma triggers, states of disconnection, attachments, and more. Once you learn how to cleanse resistance, these states will naturally loosen, and as this occurs so will the stories, beliefs, thoughts, and unprocessed emotions that have accompanied them. Right now, you might just want to get right down to business and move on to the seven steps. However, I strongly encourage you to slow down, Sally; take a breath; and really get to know how resistance is showing up.

BODILY INFLAMMATION

One of the most frequent ways resistance shows up is through bodily inflammation. If you have ever had a pinched nerve, stiff neck, headache, or back strain, you know what that can feel like. Just as eating too much sugar can cause you to break out in acne, resistance causes you to flare up in bodily tension. For me, excess bloating caused back pain. Giving up dairy helped a lot; however, I wonder how much of the inflammation was a consequence of being lied to and manipulated during the affair. Looking back, I know my body was responding to a toxic situation.

Because most of us have been trained to ignore our bodies by suppressing our feelings or pushing them away, you can see how this has led to unhealthy ways of handling strain and pressure—many of which will be discussed in Chapter 6: How Emotional Detoxes Get Sabotaged. If you don't have bodily pain, the following example illustrates how it could be there even when you aren't necessarily feeling it.

Tania had a great relationship with her mother; they seemed to get along well and enjoy each other's company. However, when I asked Tania to visualize asking her mom to discuss an uncomfortable topic, she reported that her body started to feel tight. She described her throat closing, and eventually the tension would make its way to her chest and throughout her entire body.

Just by visualizing this conversation Tania started to have a physical reaction. Tania was surprised to see this happen. This was a new way of functioning, as she never paid attention to her tension in that way. After moving through the seven steps, Tania repeated the same exercise, yet this time there was no bodily tension and she felt more open and loving toward her mom. Through our work together, Tania would discover how often she was being triggered throughout her day. This would lead to the discovery of overprocessed emotions and the link to family trauma. Noticing your bodily tension will also be an important part of your emotional detox. Here are some signs and symptoms of resistance:

- Tightness in chest
- Feeling guarded
- Holding your breath
- Clogging of the throat
- Chronic stress
- Back pain
- Neck and shoulder tension
- Shallow breathing
- Wide eyes

TRIGGERED TRAUMA

Triggered trauma happens when your body relives an unconscious memory. Unconscious memories, such as finding out about the death of a loved one, get buried in your subconscious mind. Individuals who have experienced post-traumatic stress disorder are all too familiar with this. Your brain may have a vague memory of the event; however, when it is left undigested, your body can extract the trauma. Gregg Henriques, PhD, wrote in *Psychology Today*, "as the negative emotions are inhibited and not processed, there is an increasing vulnerability that they will be triggered and released uncontrollably." Once again, some of the earliest signs of this will be through your awareness of bodily tension.

Things were going well between my husband and me. I was feeling good about our progress and how the emotional detox was serving me. My husband decided to take a trip to visit his mother. I decided to take advantage of his absence and watch a chick flick. The movie ended up being about an affair, and before I knew it, all the progress I had made up until then seemed to go right down the toilet. I was in such high reactivity that I started to believe he was going back to the affair. My entire body felt like a ball of fire, as raging, dreadful thoughts raced through my mind.

It would be about forty-eight hours before I could safely return to my body. Once again, the C.L.E.A.N.S.E. steps to the emotional detox would allow me to withdraw the heightened sense of arousal (paranoia). This is what triggered trauma does; it rattles your mind, disrupts your life, making you feel insecure and unsafe. If this happens enough times, you will start to live in an altered reality. You may begin to truly believe that something is happening when it is not. As you eliminate triggered trauma, many of the symptoms caused by it (e.g., increased heart rate, nervousness, distrust) will also be released. Triggers you can eliminate include not just those from your past but also anything you may have inherited. As we know, science now proves these reactions (e.g., bouts of anger, depression, etc.) can be passed on through the DNA, through a phenomenon known as transgenerational epigenetic inheritance.

DISCONNECTION

Disconnection happens when you become detached from your emotions. Perhaps you feel a potential threat (e.g., feeling hurt) and want to protect yourself. You deal with this by disengaging from the people or situations around you. Initially this may be a way to calm down; however, if you remain detached, your connection to your emotions will gradually decline.

Becoming detached can lead to defensive behaviors, such as appearing like you don't care, giving up, giving in, or saying something you don't mean. These responses are attempting to reveal some of your overprocessed emotions. On the surface, you might look tough, like you don't give a crap; however, underneath it all you are hurt and fearful.

Disconnection happened to Max after he had a knee injury and was forced to be out of work for quite some time. Rather than share (process) his feelings of failure, insecurity, and fear with his wife, he instead blamed her for things that were going wrong around the house. This took its toll on their marriage, leaving each of them feeling distant and resentful. His wife tried to show him how hurt she was but found he was too detached from his own feelings, let alone hers.

People will often enter states of disconnection because they believe they are bracing themselves for the worst. The challenge is that this creates social isolation, which will further suppress your most natural states of joy and love. The detox will readily weaken these tendencies, replacing them with the healing power of connection.

In my case, the disconnection from my marriage happened gradually over a long period of time. Although the affair was quite a jolt into reality, it would be through the emotional detox that the barriers and the ways both my husband and I had dealt with things would begin to fade away. If the way you think dominates your life (more so than the way you feel), honey, you may be closing yourself off. Like yo-yo dieting—one day you are on and the next day you are off—this may wreak havoc on your emotional well-being.

If you find yourself taking care of others before attending to your close relationships or you have a case of the "afters," I get it, because I did too. I thought *after* I publish the book, *after* I make dinner, *after* I have my kids squared away, *after* I lose weight, *after* I make more money, then I will spend some time connecting. The detox will help you loosen these old ways of being, and as this occurs you will be more open to replacing them with moments of connection.

ATTACHMENTS

Think of attachments as weights. Just as a physical detox may restrict your food choices, emotional attachments cramp your energy. You know you are attached if you are overfocusing on certain things such as expectations. As a result, you may feel like you can't get out of your way. You want to make better choices and sometimes can but then find yourself spinning your wheels in emotional reactivity. This is because you are leaking energy like crazy. Think of an attachment as a leaky hose. The emotions are running strong; however, the holes in the hose weaken the pressure and flow. Emotional attachments are like when we consume too much salt—they leave us feeling bloated and uncomfortable. You want to move forward, but all you can do is complain about how awful you feel.

I once worked with a client who had varicose veins. Her legs and ankles were swollen to where it negatively influenced her posture. As I tapped into the energy of her family, I received the feedback that she grew up with an excessive amount of pride. I then asked her if this was the case. Since she was from another country, she asked me to translate *pride*. I said, "Standards. Did you have high standards in your family?" Immediately she nodded her head and said, "Yes, so much. In my family there was only one way to do things, and you had to do it that way or it was wrong."

In the previous example, the family was attached to high expectations. The challenge with this mindset is emotions are controlled by outcome. If you achieve these expectations, you may initially feel good about yourself, but then you have the pressure of maintaining this level of expectation. If you fall short, you are forced to hold back or push harder. This causes you to overprocess your emotions. As you detox your attachments, this tendency will change and be replaced by a willingness to focus on your growth (no matter what) rather than attaching to your results. Here are some more signs of attachments:

- People-pleasing
- Overempathizing
- Constant need for reassurance
- Highly charged up by strong emotions (e.g., hate)
- Trying to be perfect
- Approval-seeking behavior

ABSORBED EMOTIONS

Your skin is the largest organ in your body and one of the primary ways through which you absorb toxins. Just as you can absorb the toxic chemicals from your body wash, you can also take in the emotional energy of another. If you are a parent or caregiver, you know how the sadness of your child or even a pet can often be more challenging than your own emotions. The reality is, whether the emotions stem from you or have arrived by empathizing or relating with another, they are still yours to digest and fully process. Emotional detoxes not only help you to relinquish absorbed emotions but they increase your awareness. This way you can reach out to others without running the risk of overprocessing your emotions. Instead you become emotionally resilient, increasing your capacity to engage with others without paying the price later (e.g., mental exhaustion).

During my emotional detox, I experienced quite a few restless nights. Some nights I would toss and turn while other times I would be flooded by odd dreams. In the morning my husband and I would exchange the details of our sleepless night. Before long I realized I was not only wrestling with my emotions but I could also feel his—as he could mine. It was clear we were absorbing each other's emotions.

Since sleep is one of the primary ways we process our emotions and events from the day, it was important that I allow myself to detox any absorbed emotions. The good news is whether you are detoxing over-processed emotions of your own or ones you have absorbed throughout your day, the process stays the same. You will treat every emotion as yours and allow the seven steps to guide you through the motions.

PATTERNS

A pattern is a set of consistent thoughts, behaviors, and feelings that influence the development of your personality, the characteristics that make up how you see the world. You can recognize a pattern by its predictability. If you find yourself tiptoeing around a person or a subject in attempt to control an outburst or negative reaction, then you are dancing around (and contributing to) a pattern. Patterns show up in all our relationships, not just the ones with human beings but also our relationships with emotions, food, and finances.

Here is the thing: if you want to change the template of emotional reactivity, you must change the energy. Emotional detoxes dissolve patterns by changing the energy that feeds them. Your energy is the only thing that is timeless. Your thoughts, behaviors, and histories are all based on timelines. To shift a pattern that has been rooted over a lifetime (and in some cases longer via genetics), you must choose a strategy that works both physically and temporally. Elevating your level of consciousness and tuning into energy is one way to do this.

This approach is based on quantum physics. According to Dr. Joe Dispenza in *You Are the Placebo*, "In order to change a belief or perception about yourself and your life, you have to make a decision with such firm intention that the choice carries an amplitude of energy that is greater than the hardwired programs in the brain and the emotional addiction in the body, and the body must respond to a new mind." This is what the seven steps will do for you. Not only will they get you to transform the old energy but they will also conjugate you to your most natural state of being: love. Anything less may not fully serve you.

Before moving in that direction, it is important to be clear on how patterns reveal themselves. Here are five common patterns:

1. Shifting Eyes: You are having trouble focusing your gaze. This is often a sign your body is looking to process an emotion. However, your subconscious is stuck in a pattern (a way of seeing a situation).

2. Being in the Middle: You find yourself relaying messages for someone rather than letting that person speak to the recipient directly.

3. Making Excuses: You often make up excuses for yourself and others.

4. Giving Up Needs: You are quick to give up your needs and take on the emotions and needs of others to control your discomfort.

5. Avoiding: You avoid situations, keep your true feelings secret, and engage in activities that prevent you from being present (e.g., shopping or gambling).

Patterns are a reflection of how you respond to your emotional memories. According to scientist and author Candace Pert, your emotions are stored in memory throughout your brain and body, including in your skin, glands, muscles, cells, tissue, and organs. She refers to this emotional storage system as *bodymind*. The key to releasing your emotions is to move through them consciously without judgment or shame. The steps will guide you through. Pert explained that all unexpressed emotions are good when they are given permission to be expressed. This is the goal of the detox.

Here are some things you can look forward to cleansing:

• Putting others before yourself

• Feeling like you are a burden

• Codependency

• Thoughts that you are unworthy

• Emotional debt

• Fear of loss

• Belief you are broken or sick

• Feelings of abandonment

• Judgments

Here is a snapshot of the way the energy will transform after you detox:

UNPROCESSED	PROCESSED
Doubt into	Desire
Control into	Compassion
Emotions into	Higher energy
Patterns into	Possibilities
Denying into	Allowing
Doing into	Being

CLEANSING TIP: VISUALIZE STATES OF BEING

To prepare yourself for the detox, practice visualizations. When you visualize, allow yourself to feel the experience as if it is happening. Imagine you are walking into a pond and the water is wrapped around your ankles. Visualize and feel what that would be like. Or feel your bare feet walking on the warm, soft sand with the sun shining on your back. By practicing visualizations, you are preparing your body to transform states of fear into love.

CHAPTER 4

HOW EMOTIONS GET OVERPROCESSED

"Joy and peace are my inheritance."

—A Course in Miracles

When working optimally, our bodies can absorb nutrients (raw emotions) and release toxins (reactivity). The only difference between a physical and emotional detox is the amount of resistance (reactivity). It is hard to block a physical detox (trust me, I had a colonics treatment once, and there was no opposing that); however, the way we think, what we believe, and how trauma has affected us does affect an emotional detox. Therefore, it is important to understand fully what an emotional detox is all about. The more you understand what is happening and how your whole emotions are your greatest resource, the easier the process will be.

We have all experienced those moments when we rush to get somewhere and learn we arrived...at the wrong time. Or worse yet, we misplaced our phone or wallet. When I first learned about my husband's affair, I kept forgetting why I had gone to the grocery store—entering the store used up all the energy I had for that task—because I was overprocessing emotions. To *overprocess* means we are exerting a lot of effort (energy) without gaining energy in return. As a result, we feel rushed, scattered, and unproductive. It is like burning dinner: we took the time and energy to make it, yet because it is burnt we are unable to eat it and receive the nutrients. Instead of burning food, overprocessing emotions burns out the mind, frying brain cells and bodily functions. As a result, we begin to take things personally or question our lives. *Is this job worth it? No one ever listens to me. Should I stay in this relationship? Maybe I should give up the whole idea of going back to school...* Sound familiar?

My motto is "Never make a decision when you're low-energy." If your energy is low, you are not truly processing your emotions. Here is the thing: our emotions get processed through the mindful practice of acknowledging, noticing, and tuning into our bodily sensations. But that is not all. Our emotions also get processed through our conscious and subconscious minds. I'll explain...

CONSCIOUS MIND

The conscious mind focuses on how the brain and nervous system process emotions. Both handle how we take in and send out information about the world. The conscious mind is the part of you that helps you decide if something is a potential threat. Like when a car is swerving into your lane. It is also the part of you that helps you differentiate between your likes and dislikes—what you will select from a menu, the best route to the restaurant, or what could happen if you arrive late. The conscious mind is what keeps your brain busy sorting through the possibilities and pitfalls you meet every day, like making sure you are on time for work or pick up something for dinner. The challenge is that the conscious mind tends to rely heavily on labels, putting things in categories or making decisions based on past events. Like when we decide if an idea is good or bad. The conscious mind keeps us from experiencing the present moment—the place where our emotions are truly processed—because we are busy drawing off earlier experiences to predict future events. The challenge is that all that "thinking" and "working" uses up energy. You may have experienced this type of exhaustion after having a mentally or emotionally challenging day. As we lose energy, our ability to process emotions weakens. We know this because we become less focused, more reactive, and ultimately disconnected from our bodies. In this case, our emotions can't just be poked and prodded by our minds (thinking, talking). To be able to fully process your emotions, the energy (sensations) should be allowed to be experienced through your body, which so happens to be the holder of your subconscious mind.

SUBCONSCIOUS MIND

The subconscious mind is less quantifiable than the conscious mind. One way to access it is through bodily awareness. Think of your subconscious mind as your energy body. This subtle energy body has been recognized by yogis and healers for thousands of years through mind-body practices, such as certain types of meditation, yoga, or tai chi. Science now concurs that we can influence the subconscious mind and how it affects our perceptions by directing our awareness. If we focus on our problems, debt, troubles, or disruptions, then we train our bodies to believe these things are happening even when they're not. Do this enough, like a song that gets stuck in your head, and the subconscious mind runs patterns (thoughts, beliefs, overprocessed feelings) without any effort or awareness from you.

I have often pointed out this unconscious habit to my clients—how we believe we want to have a healthy relationship, more freedom, and fun yet subconsciously have trained ourselves to abide in fear. We have invested far more attention in our reactivity than in the processing of our emotions. Undigested, feelings don't just disappear; they get stored, and one of the places they store themselves is within the body. This is one of the reasons you may feel tension or a stomachache when you focus on your problems or fears.

In her article "Negative Emotions Are Key to Well-Being" in *Scientific American*, Tori Rodriguez writes, "Even if you successfully avoid contemplating a topic, your subconscious may still dwell on it. In a 2011 study, psychologist Richard A. Bryant and his colleagues at the University of New South Wales in Sydney told some participants, but not others, to suppress an unwanted thought prior to sleep. Those who tried to muffle the thought reported dreaming about it more, a phenomenon called dream rebound." This speaks to how pushing back negative emotions and trying to be only positive may result in further consequences like emotional eating or lethargy.

This is because when digested, our emotions carry a tremendous amount of energy. It is our reaction that gets us to see them as positive or negative. It is when we embrace these sensations as whole emotions that we will begin to see them as a wellspring for joy and happiness. Once you get the hang of allowing and experiencing your emotions through the detox formula, you will be able to unleash the conscious and subconscious emotions, thoughts, and beliefs that may be inhibiting a full, free life.

During my detox, I found it difficult to be in social situations. People would ask me how I was doing, and I would offer superficial responses about my kids and their schools. Although all

PART I: TOXICITY

of that was true, what was foremost in my mind was the detox. Part of me wanted to say, "You know what I have been up to? Detoxing—that is what I am really up to." During challenging moments when I found it difficult to dive in and notice my feelings without trailing off into a story, I would anchor myself by writing in a journal or even on my phone—things like, "I feel mortified, embarrassed, judged." Then I'd redirect to the first step of the formula (Clear) by taking a walk outside to tone down reactivity.

AVOIDING

Before the detox, I must confess, there were moments in my marriage when I would hold my breath. My husband would tell me he was going to do an errand and I would think, *Thank goodness, I just need a break.* A break from feeling like he thought I wasn't enough for him. He never directly told me this, but it was how I interpreted his angst and frustrations—it was my reactivity. I later learned it was the same way he interpreted my angst and frustrations.

Once I began to follow the steps of the emotional detox, this all changed. Just as a good juice cleanse will be followed by guidance on how to transition back into eating solid foods, an emotional detox includes learning how to communicate in daily life. Yes, all those moments, when I overprocessed my emotions by ranting or commenting aloud or in my head, needed to be transformed into a healthier style of communication.

If you are dying for a break, holding your breath through the transitions of your day, desperately looking for escape, then you are overprocessing and avoiding your emotions. You might think escaping a feeling would be a way to block yourself from overprocessing, but that is not the case. When you avoid people, conversations, or conflict through behaviors such as ignoring, gossiping, distancing, drinking, texting, shopping, etc., your emotions get overprocessed because your body must exert even more energy to keep these emotions at bay. All this pushing and preventing puts invisible energetic barriers inside us. This causes us to either numb ourselves or check out both spiritually and mentally, which is what my husband did with his affair. Here is a broader list of other ways people avoid (overprocess) their emotions:

- Complaining
- Being sarcastic
- Always trying
- Worrying
- Expecting others to know what they want and need
- Taking part in drama by arguing or defending
- Rehashing the past
- Staying excessively busy
- Keeping score or a "What have you done for me lately?" attitude

TRAUMA

Another major influence on the way in which you may be overprocessing your emotions is trauma. Trauma can be experienced either directly or indirectly. It can be something that happened to you or a loved one or something that somehow changed your life in a powerful way, such as a sudden death or assault. When your body experiences strong emotions, these experiences (when left undigested) can get internalized, kind of like being emotionally memorized. The events get stored in the living cells of your body, interwoven within the history of events in your subconscious mind as memories.

Tom came to me wanting more confidence. After asking a few questions, I closed my eyes, took a deep breath (like I always do), and asked what was his lack of confidence about. I heard two words: "Sister died." It turned out he had a sister who died before he was born. Tom's mother was so distraught after the loss that she had three miscarriages. Eventually Tom was born into the family, but because of his mother's unresolved grief, he'd had a hard time truly connecting to her and therefore trusting his own feelings.

I hear these types of stories often—working through trauma takes us to the root cause of what is happening in our subconscious. Rather than hearing what people say, sometimes I must hear what they *don't say* and trust my spirit or my intuition for some guidance. I ask; I listen. Then comes the fun part: I take them through the steps of an emotional detox.

Because most of my work is focused on moving emotional energy, I knew past trauma needed to be part of the C.L.E.A.N.S.E. formula. Author Mark Wolynn confirmed that notion in his book, *It Didn't Start with You*: "Whether we inherit our parents' emotions in the womb, or they are transmitted in our early relationship with our mother, or we share them through unconscious loyalty or epigenetic changes, one thing is clear: life sends us forward with something unresolved from the past." In the case of Tom, he had a pattern of walking into a situation and closing doors. He took a yoga-teacher training course and told the instructor he was not there to learn how to teach but just to deepen his practice. Deep inside, he really did have a desire to teach, but because he was afraid it might not work out, he couldn't allow himself to feel the discomfort of letting his instructor and classmates know.

Using that example, I showed Tom how his mother's unresolved grief and trauma affected his life with an "I am not totally in or certain" attitude because he wasn't comfortable moving through his emotions. Let's face it: to go out on a limb and try something new, there is going to be some level of discomfort. Since Tom grew up watching his mother bury her own pain, he never got to experience the vulnerability to move through such emotional trauma.

When it comes to confidence, you must be "all in" or else you are merely looking for reassurance. For someone else to say "You can do it" or "Everything is going to be okay" without honoring past trauma (notice I said *honoring* not *rehashing*) doesn't help because the emotions you are holding back around the event (even if it did not happen directly to you) consume energy, making you second-guess and minimize your abilities. Wolynn wrote, "In order to process trauma, it's often helpful for clients to have a direct experience of the feelings and sensations that have been submerged in the body." This is exactly what the emotional detox is designed to do for you, and miraculously anyone who has been impacted by emotional events gets a chance to be free. *Woohoo!*

BODILY FLOW

Each time we close our eyes and breathe deeply, we are tapping into the universal flow of our life force. This force has been described in many ways—chi, energy, soul, spirit. In the emotional detox formula, the life force is connected to what already exists. Many people see it as something outside of themselves; however, the formula reminds us that this energy exists inside as well. So often we overfocus on what we don't have or wish could be better. This type of thinking and reacting clogs the connection to the life force and inhibits our ability to truly sense the movement of emotions, leading to overprocessing. As a result, you may feel stiff (attached) around certain feelings (e.g., jealousy) while detached from others (love).

What *stiff* really signals is *stuck*—when we are resistant, our energy becomes stiff, and we get stuck there. We know this because that's when we tend to overthink, causing us to protect rather than open to emotional connections, like when we treat everything as a battle and have to fight for what we need or to prove our worth. In these ways, we find ourselves working more and connecting less. When we're stuck, we are more likely to attract people who are overprocessing their emotions, reacting to the illusions *they* have created. This is where the drama comes in—relating through reacting rather than experiencing. The good news is, the moment we choose to connect to our raw emotions, we remove ourselves from that dynamic.

As we gain energy from raw emotions through emotional detox, we are likely to feel lighter, more carefree, and attentive. On the other hand, when we are overprocessing our emotions, our sensations are dull. This may create challenges we never thought of—like when senses are numbed or dim, we can become overly sensitive to noise, not just the noise in our environment but also the mental chatter in our heads. As a result, overprocessed emotions make us want to shut out the world, like a bad headache, while whole, processed emotions give us the means to be present to what is without losing energy over it.

Right now, the ability to truly process your emotions may feel remote or even impossible. I want you to trust that your body innately knows how to do this. It does it naturally with food and sleep—cleaning your body and psyche through digestion and dreams. You are not necessarily teaching your body something new but instead expanding on its capabilities. Consider the differences between overprocessing your emotions and letting them flow freely:

OVERPROCESSING	BODILY FLOW
Stuck	Connected
Dull sensations	Rich with sensations
Needing to shut out the world	Present without losing energy/reacting
Distracted	Focused, aware

When your body is preoccupied with the investment of controlling (holding back) your emotions, your awareness (energy) drops, and as this occurs your body has no choice but to defer to habits, thoughts, and patterns that deplete the energy of your emotions. The ironic part is that tension directed against what is bothering you (school, friends, work, etc.) takes the little energy you have and feeds it to the thing that is bothering you. You end up cocreating your suffering and entrench yourself in a fearful story. Trust me, I hear it all—stories of loss, unworthiness, defeat, failure, and shame. Hearing these kinds of stories makes me sad, not just about people's experiences, but because they have given away or sacrificed all their energy through overprocessed reactivity rather than listening to their bodies and receiving what their beloved raw emotions had to offer.

FEEL IT TO RECEIVE IT

If you grew up in a dysfunctional household like I did, you may have learned to act on (rather than feel) your emotions. You may have experienced people yelling, putting each other down, stuffing their emotions through silence, or being passive-aggressive by throwing out an occasional barbed comment or joke. This is how overprocessing emotions can affect families. Everyone may be doing the same thing (i.e., overprocessing their emotions), but it can manifest in different ways.

The thing is, when people react in that way rather than processing and feeling, they may believe they are managing the situation. A parent may yell at a child to get a situation under control, or a sibling may threaten a little brother to get him to stop bothering him. When several people are reacting rather than feeling their emotions, it pollutes the atmosphere of their emotions—and because these emotions must go somewhere, their bodies and minds become inflamed with excessive overprocessing, leading to high levels of anger or shame.

It isn't until we dismantle our reactions (e.g., "I am so upset") through the processing of our whole emotions that we will be able to fully be ourselves. It is important, however, that as you do this, you are clear on what reactive states look like and how they lead to overprocessing your emotions. Here are some more examples of reactive states:

- Resisting feeling or pushing away ideas because you don't agree with them

- Putting high expectations or pressure on yourself

- Thinking or talking about how upset you are

- Being quick to answer or appease others (e.g., "I am fine")

- Being resentful, wanting to get back at someone because you feel hurt

- Comparing yourself to others

- Protecting or bracing yourself for the worst

- Expecting loss or conflict

- Chronically complaining

- Shutting down or closing off

- Blaming

HOW DO YOU KNOW WHEN AN EMOTION IS PROCESSED?

The evidence that your emotions have been detoxed is likely to be subtle. I have had clients tell me they heard themselves speak up or they just felt more relaxed and confident in a relationship. The biggest thing you will feel is less attached to fear. Sure, you might connect to it here or there (you are human); however, you won't get dragged into the story and dynamic. Think about it—before you may have been negative and frustrated, but now you can be clear and hopeful.

Think of overprocessed emotions as an untended dirt road where there are unavoidable potholes and debris. In contrast, processed emotions are more like a well-paved pathway. You are still journeying through the difficulties of life, yet you are less likely to get stuck or sidetracked by the undertow of your emotions. Processed emotions allow you to take in the scenery and enjoy the ride while overprocessed emotions direct your attention to the bumps along the way.

> Jamie was suffering from severe depression. After working with her and guiding her through the emotional detox, she responded, "I feel like I am high."
>
> "High on life," I replied with a smile. Then I said, "Are you present in your body? Can you feel your surroundings?"
>
> She said, "Yes, I feel present." Then the cutest darn thing happened. She looked at the table in the room and said, "That is the most beautiful table I have ever seen," and walked out the door.

This is what happens when we fully process our emotions; we gain energy, and with that comes the ability to see the beauty around us. Our emotions are processed both consciously and subconsciously. States of disconnection, where reactivity is high, interfere with this process, leading us to either avoid or overprocess our emotions. You know your emotions are overprocessed if you feel stuck, empty, numb, or anxious. Processed emotions, on the other hand, free you from these self-limiting states of mind. Once you learn the full benefits of processing your emotions (see Chapter 2: Benefits of an Emotional Detox), you will think twice before revisiting these old patterns. Before moving on, however, it is important that you set yourself up for success by putting some things in place.

CLEANSING TIP: AROMATHERAPY

One of the quickest ways to connect your conscious and subconscious minds is through smells. As you inhale pleasing scents, this puts you into a state of relaxation and openness for processing your emotions, causing aromatherapy to be a widely appreciated healing tool. The key to aromatherapy is the scents need to be organic (just like your emotions). Companies such as Young Living are known for their organic qualities. Ideally it is best if you go with a local business or company that grows their own herbs. Aromatherapy comes in many forms, such as candles, skin oils, diffusers, eye pillows, and sprays.

CHAPTER 5

PREPARING FOR AN EMOTIONAL DETOX

"Faith is trusting God even when you don't understand His plan."

—Joel Osteen

The time following the revelation of my husband's affair was filled with trepidation. I turned over every pebble and boulder—focusing on details and big things I had been stuffing away for years. In the back of my mind, I couldn't help but wonder, "How the fuck did this happen?" On the surface, it may seem like I had no time to prepare for an emotional detox, that I was blindsided, and that it was too late for me to come up with a plan, because when we get slammed with reactivity, the last thing we need is to worry about carrying out some sort of plan. During those challenging times, you have two choices: sit in reactivity or heal. The journey begins with a decision to heal. Not just the fresh but also the old scars.

With that said, structure is beneficial. The suggestions in this chapter provide just that. You will be introduced to the detox mindset on a physical level, as well as things to put into place to get your emotional energy moving in a productive way. Since most of us have never been taught about emotional detox, it is important that you are thoroughly prepared. Otherwise, you may find yourself going through the motions and not seeing changes.

THE DETOX MINDSET

Emotional detoxes are a practice like meditation, chanting, or tai chi. To master the technique, you must commit to the practice. Like meditation, emotional detox is a mindful way to move through processing your emotions so that you learn, grow, and transform your experiences. To support myself in the practice, I developed the mindset that my emotions were a treat rather than a form of treatment. In my mind, putting small actions into place was a way to cultivate the ideal physical and mental environment for an emotional detox. Think of your body as an aquarium—to have healthy, flourishing fish, the toxins need to be removed from the water or else the fish will get sick. Since our bodies are about 60 percent water, it is important that you too take some actions to create a nourishing emotional atmosphere for your detox.

When I was hit with the news of the affair, I found myself walking blindly through the crisis. I was resistant to therapy at first because it felt conditional—like I had to do things or think a certain way to be empowered or healed. Looking back, it wasn't necessarily the therapy I was resisting, it was that something inside me knew my healing— the emotional detox, which I was already researching—would be different. My husband and I did eventually work with an excellent therapist, but as an individual, I found the detox to be enough, and my realizations helped me structure and fine-tune the formula. Part of that process was learning how to prepare for an emotional detox.

Since most of the suggestions in this chapter produce a healthier lifestyle (even before the detox), you are likely to feel better right away. This is important because, like a juice detox, the better you feel, the more likely you are to stick with the program. Sure, there may be days you skip or skimp on the process. I remember going to the gym feeling like a hot mess and leaving after ten minutes. If this occurs, go easy on yourself and move to one of the simpler suggestions like drinking water.

Try to implement two or three (or more) of the following suggestions *before* moving through the C.L.E.A.N.S.E. steps.

PREPARATION

Some physical detoxes absolutely prohibit certain foods while others are more lenient—there are variations based on the goal and the individual. Since we are all different, our emotional detoxes won't look quite the same. The nine suggestions that follow focus on the physical side of the seven steps, whereas C.L.E.A.N.S.E. will help you mindfully integrate the more spiritual aspects of the detox.

ONE: DAILY MOVEMENT

If you are not crazy about cardio, join the club—neither am I. But you can take a brisk walk, run with your dog, do some jumping jacks, spin on a bike, or take an aerobics class. However, just as with a physical detox, making time for movement during an emotional one is essential. When your heart rate goes up, your blood begins to circulate through your major detoxifying organs like your kidneys and liver, helping you to remove toxins (things like heavy metals and BPA found in plastic). This circulation is key to your emotional well-being because it significantly decreases symptoms of anxiety, making it easier for you to tone down reactivity.

You may have noticed your body adjusts its temperature according to your physical movement. The more you run, the warmer you get. Your body then begins to regulate its temperature through sweating. The same thing happens with emotions. A higher level of reactivity can have an impact on your body temperature. The more movement in our emotions, the warmer we may feel, whereas less movement (emotionally) can make us feel cooler. This affects the expansion and contraction of your muscles. Anger, for example, can have quite a bit of movement—producing heat in your face and making you feel like your veins are going to burst—while heavier emotions such as depression can make you feel cold, drained, and lifeless.

Incorporating daily movement helps keep energy moving, stimulating fluctuations in your bodily temperature necessary for detoxifying emotions. As your body temperature heats up or cools down, this reflects what is happening internally with your emotions. For example, sadness may bubble up and expand, and as the reactivity is released, you get to download the pure energy of that emotion. Tell yourself there is something wrong or panic, and you will interrupt the process. I'll get into this further in Chapter 6: How Emotional Detoxes Get Sabotaged, but for now remember to keep things moving because when you do apply the seven steps, your body will be more willing to release any resistance.

Start where you can! Those of you who don't exercise at all might be rolling your eyes now. You might be saying, "Been there, done that." I say, "Baloney!" You haven't done it in this way. Sure, you might have exercised because you wanted to lose weight, gain muscle, relieve stress, or just feel better; however, this time it's different. Your intention is to connect to your wholeness. If you are one of those people who needs some real guidelines, I would say plan on incorporating an exercise program for at least a few weeks and begin where you can. Some simple ways to add activity can be taking the stairs instead of the elevator, parking farther away from your destination, or taking frequent breaks (standing up, stretching, swaying your arms) at your desk. Ideally it would be great if you could work yourself up to thirty minutes of various exercises four to five days a week. There is evidence that having to meet someone for a walk or joining a class can help get you motivated. For those of you who are going through some sort of a crisis, believe me, I get it—there were days I went to the gym and stared at the wall. Then there were days I just lay in bed. Eventually, with practice, the seven steps allowed me to progress further in my emotional healing (wholeness), as they will for you.

TWO: HYDRATE

When you are dehydrated, it can cause symptoms such as headaches, anxiety, fatigue, clogged pores, insomnia, and mental confusion. During my detox, I drank a lot of coconut water and ate fruits and veggies that are high in water content, like melons, zucchini, celery, and spinach. You know you are well hydrated if your urine is pale yellow or clear. If it is dark and has a strong odor, you will have a challenging time digesting and absorbing your food and your raw emotions.

Dr. Laura Koniver wrote in her article "The Healthiest Ways to Release Any Stuck Emotions" that staying well hydrated is one way to release sorrow, worry, and grief. She states, "When the energy is flowing through your body, you are releasing the old and welcoming in the new and *healing happens effortlessly*. In fact, that is what happens when the energy flows through your body: it gives rise to emotions...emotions are the body's energetic release valve." Staying hydrated will help keep your body's energy flowing steadily.

If you are not a big fan of drinking water, consider pampering yourself by putting fresh fruit in a pitcher (strawberry, kiwi, or lemon slices) and allowing it to infuse your water with some nutrients. You can also buy a cool water bottle, one that helps you to know exactly how much you drink. Personally I like hot water with lemon. Keep in mind anything with carbonation does not count because carbonated and caffeinated beverages (even green tea) can interfere with the digestive process. You will learn in the seven-step C.L.E.A.N.S.E. formula how your colon plays a role in supporting your emotional flow.

THREE: PROBIOTICS

Taking probiotics either as a drink (I love kombucha) or in capsule form (usually found in the refrigerator section at health food stores) is a way to consume healthy bacteria that will help you remove toxins. Mixing one tablespoon of organic apple cider vinegar with a glass of water is one of the more affordable ways to do this.

If you are still on the fence about taking probiotics, here is some insight on how your gut and emotions are connected. Your gastrointestinal tract starts (like a tube) at your mouth and ends at your anus. According to the article "How Probiotics Can Transform Your Emotional Response" by Mary Toscano, "Research findings show that the bacteria in the gut can influence the brain and consequently, these emotions link gut bacteria to depression, anxiety, as well as other disorders." In addition, Siri Carpenter, PhD, states in the article "That Gut Feeling," published in *Monitor on Psychology*, "Just as gut bacteria affect the brain, the brain can also exert profound influences on the gut microbiome—with feedback effects on behavior. Numerous studies, for example, have shown that psychological stress suppresses beneficial bacteria."

In the article, Carpenter also reports that studies have shown a positive impact on reducing levels of stress and anxiety in mice when introducing a probiotic. The research being done so far shows great promise for those who suffer from anxiety, depression, Crohn's disease, and gastrointestinal problems.

If probiotics can curb social anxiety (which can be intense), they could certainly help move emotional turmoil. Even when I'm not doing an emotional detox, I continue to use probiotics two to three times per week and have found many benefits, such as a decrease in allergies, brighter skin, and more regular bowel movements.

FOUR: LIMIT DAIRY

Before the detox, I was a cheese girl. I would buy an entire block, cut it up into pieces, and eat them mindlessly while I worked. What I wasn't taking seriously were the multiple studies linking dairy to mood instability and depression. I had always toyed with the idea of substituting dairy with other foods, and knowing I tend to hold my stress in my stomach area, it seemed natural to remove it from my food choices to support the detoxification of my emotions.

Evidence shows it is not the dairy per se that is the problem but the way it is produced. One of the concerns is the added hormones, which for an adolescent or a menopausal woman (like me) can wreak havoc on the digestive and nervous systems. One of the side effects of dairy (like stress) is it produces mucus (which contains toxins our bodies want to get rid of and which, when not cleared, can cause weight gain, acne, and phlegm, making us more susceptible to allergies and other inflammatory issues). I often picture the mucus coating the reactivity (toxins), making it difficult to digest my emotions.

Almond and coconut milk products are great substitutes. When fortified, each offers you the calcium without the bloating and gassiness dairy can cause.

Soy products are a subject of debate. Clinical nutritionist Kimberly Snyder writes in her book *The Beauty Detox Foods* that some soy products can depress your thyroid function and that soybeans are one of the foods most heavily sprayed with pesticides. Certainly the choice is yours; however, I think you will find whole-food calcium alternatives such as kale, almonds, and spinach are a great source for supporting you in your wholeness journey.

FIVE: MINIMIZE ALCOHOL CONSUMPTION

Alcohol and drugs such as marijuana will negatively interfere with your emotional atmosphere. If drinking a glass of wine or having a beer is a way for you to wind down at the end of the day, you may want to consider some alternatives. For many this will be quite a challenge, but both marijuana and alcohol depress emotions. They have a way of lowering our level of consciousness so that we are less aware of our bodily sensations. To truly detox your emotions (reactivity), you must have bodily awareness. This is not to say you can't have an occasional glass of wine with dinner; however, if you are consuming more than a couple of glasses a week, you may not get the full benefits of the detox.

As I've helped clients move their emotions through energy work, I've seen that they might feel better in the short term even when continuing to drink alcohol; however, the habit of consuming alcohol to wind down will slowly counteract any progress. If you are having difficulty stopping yourself from this habit, you are going to want to get support. You are likely to find the community of people looking to change their drinking and drug-use habits quite supportive, encouraging, and friendly. Groups such as Alcoholics Anonymous and Refuge Recovery have safe, comfortable ways to successfully help members.

SIX: CLEAN UP YOUR FOOD

As during a physical detox, consuming whole foods during an emotional detox is extremely beneficial. This is because whole foods support the energy of your emotions. Nutritional coaches such as Tammi Smith, whom I have had the privilege of partnering with to create emotional detox programs, advocates for whole (unprocessed), clean eating. This means you will be selecting foods that are closest to their most natural (whole and organic) state—foods that are low in sodium, sugar, dyes, and processing. You may consider replacing white-flour products with quinoa bread, quinoa pasta, or quinoa rice. It is important that you eat regular meals and snacks. There were times I was too busy for lunch and as a result slipped into reactivity in the form of nervousness, but I found that keeping nuts and fruit handy for snacking helped.

You will want to eat a variety of foods such as fruits, veggies, grains, nuts, etc. You can also add nutrient-rich chia or hemp seeds to your salads or sandwiches. Both are high in omega-3 fatty acids (healthy fats), which are good for your brain, and have antioxidant and anti-inflammatory properties as well. (Remember, inflammation can be caused by excessive emotional stress.) Here are some wholesome, clean foods to consider putting on your shopping list:

- Quinoa breads, pastas, cereals, and rice
- Avocados, spinach, and kale (for calcium)
- Apple cider vinegar to make dressing for salads
- Coconut water (for hydration)
- Nuts (especially almonds)
- Healthy fats, such as coconut oil, olive oil, and butter
- Lean meats, such as chicken (preferably no added hormones)
- Coconut or almond milk
- Fruits high in calcium, such as kiwis, strawberries, oranges, and prunes
- Foods high in dopamine, the neurotransmitter for elevating mood, such as bananas, dark chocolate, and turmeric (which is great on salads and sandwiches)

SEVEN: REDUCE DISTRACTIONS AND EXTRA RESPONSIBILITIES

During the next several months it is important that you focus on your healing journey, and that means limiting distractions and extra responsibilities. This is not the time to host the annual family reunion or volunteer in your child's classroom. The concern is that you will begin to use these tasks as an excuse to not care for your emotional needs. Give yourself at least six months before taking on something new. Unless you are miserable or in an abusive situation, this is not a time to make rash decisions or keep up with traditions just for the sake of habit.

Also keep in mind too much gossip, social media, and texting can distract you from your intention to connect to your whole emotions. Here is the thing: when you distract yourself from what is happening in the moment, you never allow yourself to process your emotions. Distractions keep you from receiving the energy, wisdom, and strength your emotions can offer. For the next six months, try to minimize your exposure to distractions. If you check your social media hourly, space this out and check in at the beginning, middle, and (if necessary) end of the day. I removed all social media apps from my phone, which meant I had to be sitting at my computer to check social media.

EIGHT: REQUEST AND ACCEPT HELP

Here comes the hard part. To truly support the emotional atmosphere of your detox, you are going to have to be willing to both ask for and accept help. As I am writing this, my husband has just left to drive one of our daughters to the bus stop. In the past, I would have said I would do it to give him more time to get ready for work, but I realize how immature my thinking was. Allowing him to spend time with his daughter and do simple daily tasks is a way to nourish the inner landscape of emotional connection.

As you prepare for your emotional detox, I want you to challenge yourself. Say yes to receiving support and then reflect upon and ask for what you need. It may be as simple as asking for clarification on something that was said, telling someone you could use a hug, or receiving a gesture of kindness. You never know how it will arrive. It could be simply a stranger holding the door for you or a teacher taking a little extra time to answer your questions. This is your time to be in the practice of asking for and receiving emotional energy.

NINE: SLEEP

As a psychology professor, I find it interesting to learn about how much sleep college students get in proportion to their stress level about homework, how they have been suffering from insomnia for years, or how the time spent on their phones outweighs the amount of sleep they get. I tell them that sleep is the way our bodies download the emotions of the day. Without a consistent and adequate amount, we run the risk of overprocessing our emotions. On average, adults need a minimum of seven to eight hours of sleep a day.

To prepare yourself for the detox, it will be important to prioritize your sleep for a while. If this doesn't seem possible, then consider putting in some time to just relax without the TV, phone, or computers. Read a book, drink noncaffeinated tea (see the Additional Resources to Increase Emotional Flow section at the end of this book), or listen to some calming music before you go to bed. Sit outside in the sun or take a little catnap. These little things, when done mindfully, can make a big difference in your detox experience.

HOW LONG IS IT GOING TO TAKE?

C.L.E.A.N.S.E. is a lifestyle, and once you get the hang of it, it will take only three to five minutes each day. When you begin, I recommend learning and practicing the steps once a day for a minimum of ninety days. This gives you enough time to memorize the process, feel the benefits, and develop the practice. Keep in mind that this formula does far more than meets the eye!

After the ninety-day period you will have a good sense of what it feels like to digest your raw emotions. There will be times you'll find yourself reacting and need to redirect yourself to Step 1 (Clear), but it should feel quite natural.

Let's face it, stress is part of life and some of it is necessary to keep you safe (e.g., dodging an oncoming car). The idea is to develop a relationship with the C.L.E.A.N.S.E. steps and find ways to integrate them into your life, like with your morning cup of coffee, in your parked car before work, or during exercise. Most of all, let go of the results. If you find yourself discouraged, use the formula to dissolve this emotion. Soon you will see how that works.

DOES AGE MATTER?

Since an emotional detox is a mindful practice of tuning in and honoring and respecting your emotions, you can begin teaching and modeling it at any age. Babies are born into the world already sensing, exploring, and feeling their raw emotions. As I've mentioned, your emotions are what you are born with; reactivity is what you learn.

How you respond to children's emotions is the way in which they begin to learn about their feelings. Rushing to quiet their cries or telling them to squelch their anger may send a message that emotions are bad or disruptive and are therefore meant to be pushed away or ignored. This is not to say parents shouldn't guide their children in socially acceptable ways of expression, but we don't have to act on our anger, sorrow, or disappointment to feel it. In Step 5 (Nourish), you will learn skills that allow you to create an emotionally whole atmosphere within your home and relationships.

I worked with an adolescent boy who was injured and had to sit out his sports season. This was difficult for him because he was one of the star players. On the surface it looked like he was having a bad start to the year; however, on the inside there was something new to be discovered. He had been identified as an athlete—the label others gave him—and when he could no longer play, he lost a sense of who he was. I taught him how his expectations for himself, as well as how he expected others to see him, were a form of reactivity. Once he understood, he could digest and receive the fullness of his raw emotions (fear) in his experience.

Here is the thing about reactivity: people get used to us being a certain way. Whether we are a sports star, frazzled mother, or cynical boss, people begin to see us as our reactivity. We may even begin to believe this ourselves. Within every reaction are overprocessed emotions waiting to be embraced, and as they are, we begin to see ourselves and others differently.

CLEANSING TIP: MANTRAS

Mantras are sounds, syllables, and words that are repeated. To help both prepare and support yourself through the detox, consider reciting this mantra aloud, ten times in a row, daily for forty days: *Now that I am willing and ready to receive the energy of my emotions, all possibilities are in motion. Thank you.*

PART II
THE C.L.E.A.N.S.E. FORMULA

SEVEN STEPS TO AN EMOTIONAL DETOX

WHEN PEOPLE ARE GOING THROUGH A CHALLENGING TIME, THEY TEND TO GRAB FOR ANYTHING WITHIN REACH. THEY TOY WITH DIFFERENT STRATEGIES AND SUPPORTS, HOPING TO FIND THE MAGIC ONE. THE DETOX FORMULA PUT TOGETHER IN THE C.L.E.A.N.S.E. PROGRAM IS NOT ONE TECHNIQUE BUT INSTEAD A BLEND OF HIGHLY CONSCIOUS, SELF-AWARE STRATEGIES COMBINED INTO ONE SENSIBLE AND LIVABLE FORMULA. THE DETOX IS MADE UP OF SEVEN STEPS:

1. Clear

2. Look Inward

3. Emit

4. Activate Joy

5. Nourish

6. Surrender

7. Ease

I've dedicated a section to each step, offering you a deeper understanding of not only why the steps work but how. Please remember, this is not about doing the steps; the goal of the formula is to gain a relationship with your energy and hence your emotions. Keep in mind you are dissolving reactivity, which has led to the overprocessing of your emotions. Embrace them whole and you will soon connect to joy.

> The C.L.E.A.N.S.E. steps saved my life. The pain in my heart lasted way longer than anything I had anticipated. I must confess, I totally get why people turn to drugs. There were days I might have been tempted to pop a pill had someone offered me some. Sure, there were moments when I felt hopeful, and glimpses of happiness would sneak in. However, they didn't seem to stick. That is until I stepped foot on this same path I am about to share with you.

You may have heard about the "law of attraction," which is based on the concept that what you focus on will expand and be drawn into your life (positive or negative). The steps work in conjunction with this law; however, what I have found is that if there is reactivity in your body, this can spoil your efforts even if you are focusing on the positive. This is because you are ignoring your ability to read and receive the energy of your emotions. Once you strengthen this ability (through the steps), you will be more in sync with connecting to joy, and as this occurs, something cool happens: you realize love is all there is. When reactivity is truly released, there is no negative, bad, or worse—you won't be able to connect with that mindset because you are in a state of love and possessing the power of non-effort. Love and free will are what brought you here (into a physical body) and happen to be what will set you free. Your raw emotions connect you to this path.

Although there are seven steps, the process, once learned and put into practice, will take only a few minutes each day. Of course, wanting to know how long it will take *is* a reaction. See how easily it slips in?

Now, let's begin.

C.L.E.A.N.S.E. STEP 1: CLEAR

*"Our job is to love others without stopping to inquire
whether or not they are worthy."*

—Thomas Merton

When our desk is chaotic and cluttered, our natural urge is to organize papers, books, and supplies to clear the way for work. Otherwise, we'll be distracted. When it comes to an emotional detox, I apply the same principle. The last thing we want to do is leave our emotions in a messy stack or hide them in a drawer. We remove thoughts, fears, and behaviors—the distractions from the work of noticing sensations. That's why *clearing* is the first step in the C.L.E.A.N.S.E. formula.

Neuroscience shows us that when cortisol—the stress hormone—is triggered and elevated, the synaptic connections that allow nerve cells to send and receive information are suppressed and the plasticity of our brains—our ability to learn and change—is diminished. When we are reacting or in a state of fight-flight-freeze, it is difficult to change our energetic patterns within our bodies and therefore our minds. It's easier to evolve when we're calm.

Think about it—when we are learning to drive, if our teacher is anxious and critical, we are more likely to stiffen up. Our shoulders and neck might get tight, and as this occurs our level of confidence and reassurance decreases. There were several times during the first part of my emotional detox when I started to doubt my ability to move through the situation with my husband. I'd wonder: *Is this for real? Will things be different? Is it just going to happen again?* The more I questioned, the tenser I became. These thoughts didn't stop until I coached myself by saying, "Sheri, you are on an emotional detox, this is not about him, don't get sidetracked—stick with the program." Treating myself in this way opened the doorway to the steps, allowing healing to begin.

SEEING WHERE YOU'RE STUCK

Patterns are predictable ways of functioning, and not all of them are bad, but when we're trapped in one that's not working, it's almost impossible to make progress. Recognizing patterns of reactivity is a way to interrupt them and lay the groundwork for a better, happier, more productive state of being. The best way to do this and begin the clearing process is to look within ourselves and accept things for what they are—to acknowledge we are stuck in a pattern. Do we have a "default" mode of thinking about a person or situation? We may think someone is distant or too stressed out to connect, so we fall into patterns, like I did, of working too hard or ignoring our feelings.

When it comes to clearing pathways and redirecting our energy, it's important to pinpoint how we both hold back and push through emotions. It's like driving to work a different way—it may take some time to become familiar with the new route, so we should pay extra attention until our mind and body move through the process with ease. As you practice the C.L.E.A.N.S.E. steps, remember that raising our level of awareness (instead of our effort) strengthens our ability to notice.

Here are some patterns of reactivity I've seen in myself and my clients:

- You avoid speaking up because you are worried you might make the situation worse.

- You put your emotions "on hold," waiting for a better time to feel them and end up leaving them to fester.

- You make excuses for behavior instead of uncovering the source of that behavior.

- You have a difficult time asking for help, admitting a mistake, or letting people know how you feel.

- When you voice your opinion, you can't shake the sensation that you've done something wrong or bad.

Take Susan. She couldn't break her pattern of letting her mother-in-law's unsolicited advice or comments—like "When I was raising my kids, that never would have happened under my watch"—get under her skin. Susan tried to be patient, but every encounter left her drained and frustrated, and the toxic relationship had a negative impact on her partner and children. This began to change when I coached Susan on how to read her reactivity. I explained that if she noticed doing things such as tensing her lips and squinting her eyes in response to her mother-in-law's comments, she would see she was stuck in a pattern of holding back her energy by swallowing her breath rather than expanding with it.

Most of us have been trained to look at behavior through how a person speaks and acts. Based on what we see, we decide (without ever asking) how this person feels and thinks. In the previous example, Susan decided her mother-in-law was critical and pushy based on her comments. As a result, Susan's body began to go into a pattern of defensiveness. I see this all the time in clients.

What Susan and many of us don't recognize is that overprocessed emotions underlie comments such as those from Susan's mother-in-law. They are a way to control or push away what we are feeling, making it about them, not us. The way we find patterns is to watch ourselves. Notice what is happening when you are in a state of reactivity—your body language, thoughts, stories, and most of all your breathing. Are you holding your breath, clenching your fists, or nodding your head? These are some physical signs to notice when you are picking up on a pattern.

Once we have revealed our pattern, the next step is to figure out the levels and scope within that pattern by reading reactivity.

READING REACTIVITY

As you are noticing patterns, you are beginning to learn how to read reactivity. Like learning a foreign language, this takes time and practice. Only instead of learning sounds, words, and meanings you are practicing the skill of self-observation with nonjudgment. The moment you begin to judge yourself, you are no longer reading reactivity; instead you are in it. If you notice you are holding back from what you want to say or you are unsure how to approach a topic, this would be a sign that you are reading (observing) reactivity. If you take it a step further and start to judge the person in front of you, create a story in your head, or tell yourself how crummy you feel, you are no longer observing but are *in* reactivity.

There were many occasions when my stress levels would interfere with my ability to process information. My husband would try to check in with me about things. He was diligent about asking if something was okay with me. I had the habit of answering him without thinking. "Sure, that's fine," I would say. Hours later I would begin to process what he had asked me and how I'd responded. Wait a minute—what did he say? Crap! Why didn't I give myself a chance to think about it? It wasn't until I was able to honor and explain to my husband how I was having trouble processing and request he give me the details again that this pattern began to change.

Not being aware of such patterns can waste a lot of energy. This is because when you are not processing your emotions, it is likely that you are not thinking clearly. You might say something you don't mean and then spend the rest of your day trying to make up (gain energy) from it. Rather than focus on what you did, instead I encourage you to tune in to (observe) your reactivity levels. People assume you must be smarter and have a higher intelligence to think more clearly. What they are not taking into account is that your intelligence goes far beyond your brain.

In *What Are You Hungry For?*, Deepak Chopra writes, "Being an observer is the same as getting out of the way, and when you get out of the way, you give the mind-body connection space to rest and readjust." This might seem like a tall order. Maybe you believe your life is way too complicated to observe without reactivity. Believe me, I felt the same way. The C.L.E.A.N.S.E. steps will strengthen your ability to do this.

The easiest way to read reactivity is to notice the quality of your thoughts. The more fearful or hopeless they are in nature, the higher the level of reactivity. However, if you are having suicidal thoughts, don't take these steps alone. You can still practice them, but be sure to have a professional in your life before getting started. I never had suicidal thoughts per se; however, I did gain an understanding of how someone may get to that point—how it is all a cry for help, and unfortunately some of those cries are well hid until after the fact.

What you will see when you observe reactivity is the quality, speed, and nature of your thoughts. This gives insight into the degree of reactivity. I always picture it like a gas stove: the flames can move from simmer (low) to full blast (high). A high flame would mean high levels of reactivity, while a low flame would mean you are calm.

The following chart gives you a better idea of this range. The purpose of the chart is to increase your awareness of reactivity, not just for yourself but also for others. Once you learn to notice when people are having a high level of reactivity, rather than get sucked into their drama, you will have compassion for them. This was huge for me. If someone close to me was in high reactivity, I would label it as such and recognize that it is a hard place to be.

LOW LEVEL OF REACTIVITY	MEDIUM LEVEL OF REACTIVITY	HIGH LEVEL OF REACTIVITY
You have a positive outlook on things.	You are calm; however, you are more interested in what is going on outside of you (e.g., gossip) than inside.	You have irrational thoughts, which include words like *nobody*, *everyone*, *should*, *you*, and *can't*.
You focus on the big picture rather than getting hung up on the details. Even when slightly annoyed or offended you stay on task.	You are forgetful and distracted and wander off task. You feel tired, frustrated, and/or drained by day-to-day annoyances.	You are unable to stay on task and forget things like appointments and birthdays. You call in sick to work or consider impulsive "outs" like quitting your job or leaving your marriage.

LOW LEVEL OF REACTIVITY	MEDIUM LEVEL OF REACTIVITY	HIGH LEVEL OF REACTIVITY
When you are aware that you are not in the moment, you find ways to redirect yourself (e.g., deep breathing).	You are fluctuating between the past, present, and future. You find yourself thinking about the same things over and over.	You are fearful of the future and stuck in the past.
You use "I" messages ("I feel…"). You are uninterested in reactivity and interested in digesting and expressing your whole emotions.	You don't use "I" messages. You are negative, and you vent and complain.	You find fault in others or yourself but hold back from expressing your feelings. You try to protect other people's feelings through behaviors like people-pleasing but ignore your own feelings.
You take care of yourself (e.g., exercise, eat well, get enough sleep). You notice your body, its levels of reactivity, and follow the C.L.E.A.N.S.E. steps.	You feel conflicted about taking care of yourself.	Taking care of yourself comes with too much guilt to even try. You neglect nutrition and exercise and ignore bodily signals (even exhaustion and dehydration).

THE VAGUS NERVE

Once you acknowledge your level of reactivity, you will then stimulate your vagus nerve. The vagus nerve is the longest cranial nerve, extending from your brain stem to your abdomen. The vagus nerve connects to multiple organs such as your heart, lungs, liver, kidneys, spleen, fertility organs, and pancreas. It also affects your neck, ears, and tongue. Your vagus nerve has a direct impact on your parasympathetic nervous system, which helps put your body at ease so you can properly digest not only your food but also your emotions. When your vagus nerve is not being stimulated, it is referred to as "being low." According to the article "32 Ways to Stimulate Your Vagus Nerve (and Symptoms of Vagal Dysfunction)" on SelfHacked.com, "Studies have found that higher vagal tone is associated with greater closeness to others and more altruistic behavior." On the other hand, low vagal tone can contribute to multiple disorders, such as anxiety, intestinal problems, depression, and eating disorders.

When you stimulate your vagus nerve, the relationship between your brain and body strengthens. One way to stimulate it is by increasing your blood flow. As the blood flow through your brain, organs, and gut increases, your body will learn to relax, soften, and fully digest its emotions. The connection between your gut and emotions will be explained further in the Emit step. For now, your focus is to stimulate your vagus nerve. Here are some ways to do this:

- Exercise
- Singing loudly, chanting aloud
- Yoga
- Prayer
- Splashing cold water or putting ice cubes on your face
- Deep diaphragmatic breathing (described in the next step)
- Positive social interactions

- Meditation

- Laughter

- Hugging (pressing your chest against another's)

The intention is to stimulate the vagus nerve and calm your sympathetic (fight-or-flight) nervous system. I find when dealing with emotional trauma or medium to high levels of reactivity, it can be difficult to go right into deep breathing. By choosing to stimulate your vagus nerve first, your body will be more open to taking deeper breaths. I suggest you do exercises to stimulate your vagus nerve daily, as part of your self-care routine. You can also implement them during times of stress or when you notice that your breathing is shallow.

After I label my level of reactivity, here are three exercises I like to do.

RESET THE VAGUS NERVE

Each morning I sit in my chair, take a couple sips of coffee, and begin Step 1—clearing reactivity—by resetting my vagus nerve. Naturopath and coach Cheryl Townsley does a great job of explaining this technique on her website, but in case you're limiting your computer time, this is how to do it:

- Place the index and middle fingers of your right hand above your navel, and press to the right and inward.

- Take these same two fingers and press in above your navel and then again to the left. Then press in to the right, middle, and left (about an inch above the navel).

- With the other hand, simultaneously push the pads of three fingers into your scalp on top of your head (at the back), then press your fingers to the middle of your scalp (on top of your head), and then to the front (just above the forehead).

- Do the process simultaneously with one hand pressing points just above the navel and the other hand pressing the top of your head. Repeat three times, bring your arms down to your sides at the end, close your eyes, and breathe.

- You will notice your breath become deeper, your jaw release, your neck feel looser, and your shoulders shift away from your ears. If you don't notice anything, try again.

FEAR TAP

In *The Little Book of Energy Medicine*, author Donna Eden describes a technique called "the fear tap." It calms the fight-or-flight response, reduces irrational fear, and steadies your mind. First you flip one of your hands over so the palm is facing down. With your other hand, take your fingers and press on the back side of your hand, halfway between your wrist and fingers, between your ring finger and pinkie finger. Tap this area with two or three fingers for thirty to sixty seconds, breathing in through your nose and out through your mouth.

CAT AND COW STRETCH

The cat and cow stretch is something I do often. It is a yoga asana that is one of the most refreshing ways to stimulate your vagus nerve. Here is a seated version. Sit on the edge of a chair with your feet about hip-width apart. Place your hands on your thighs, and as you exhale, round your spine like a scared cat, tucking your chin in toward your chest. Then inhale, open your spine, and draw your heart forward while you bring your shoulder blades back. Inhale (open your heart) and exhale (squeeze your core rounding forward). Allow your breathing to create more flexibility in your spine.

Larry had a history of moving into the freeze response during social situations. He was fine with one or two people, but as the group became larger, Larry would begin experiencing shortness of breath, nervousness, and irrational thoughts. Rather than enjoy the company, instead he would focus on how to make a quick yet graceful exit. Practicing the three previous exercises allowed him to be more fully connected to his body, helping him to feel safe and secure.

HANDS ON FOREHEAD

Another way to reduce reactivity is by rubbing your hands together vigorously for about ten seconds and then placing one palm on your forehead and the other hand on top of the hand already on your forehead. It will look like you are checking your head for a fever. By placing your hands in this position, closing your eyes for thirty seconds, and breathing into your lower belly, you are pulling the blood up to the forebrain. As this occurs, reactivity reduces. You'll know this because once you take your hands away (placing them palm down on your lap), your breathing will come from your lower abdomen.

SCAN

Once you acknowledge your level of reactivity, do one more quick whole body scan. The way a copy machine scans from one end of a piece of paper to the other, you will scan your body with your awareness. Keep your eyes closed or softly open, begin at the top of your head, and move all the way to the bottom of your feet. Scanning your body is like preheating your oven. Your oven needs to be a certain temperature to cook your food properly inside and out; likewise, your body needs to be a certain way—i.e., cleared of reactivity—in order to assimilate your whole emotions.

Clearing reactivity is best done in the morning because when you sleep your body is digesting the stressors of the day. If you have ever woken up out of sorts or wondering what all your dreams were about, you know what I mean. It is important to begin the day clearing the reactivity that may have surfaced overnight.

Go ahead and take a moment now to do a full ten-second scan:

1. Sit or stand up straight with your arms down by your sides and your feet parallel on the floor.

2. Inhale.

3. On the exhale, using your awareness, slowly trace from the top of your head to the soles of your feet.

RECAP

- Cleanse pathways by acknowledging reactivity as low, medium, or high.

- Tone your vagus nerve and reduce your fight-or-flight response, moving through the fear tap/acupressure technique, cat and cow stretch, and/or the "hands on forehead" exercise.

- End with a ten-second body scan.

- Move on to Step 2.

CLEANSING TIP: PATTING CHEST

When babies or small children are upset, an instinctual response is to pat or rub their back (the back of their heart). When you find yourself rattled or reactive, acknowledge this tension in your body by gently patting or tapping the front of your heart center. Say to yourself, "Calm down, everything is going to be okay." Do this for a minute while closing your eyes. Notice how your body will respond by taking some deeper, fuller breaths. You are on your way to becoming more centered and grounded.

C.L.E.A.N.S.E. STEP 2: LOOK INWARD

*"The Lord says, 'Forget what happened before and
don't think about the past. Look at
the new thing I am going to do. It is already
happening. Don't you see it?'"*

—Isaiah 43:18–19

Looking inward promotes the skill of developing self-awareness. This is different than self-reflection. Self-reflection is when you focus on your thoughts and actions, whereas self-awareness is when you witness your feelings. One is not better than the other. Both are essential for helping you move toward your growth edge. Looking inward is about transitioning your attention from self-reflection to self-awareness. It is during this transition that your thoughts are likely to intrude on your process. In this step, you will learn the difference between self-reflection and self-awareness, when and how your ego steps in, ways to settle into your body, the skill of body dialoguing, how noticing and listening to your body heals you, and why it is important to step up your game.

As a yoga teacher, I watch people fluctuate between self-reflection and self-awareness all the time. As I guide them through the practice, I can see them mentally positioning themselves into certain poses, placing their hands and feet, and I see their awareness as they follow my directions. As they sit in various poses, it is clear which people are still in their heads (self-reflecting), fidgeting their way through the process. I remind them to soften and allow themselves to become a witness to their breathing—this is the process of developing self-awareness. The following chart illustrates the difference between self-reflection and self-awareness. Again, both are necessary for looking inward.

SELF-REFLECTION	SELF-AWARENESS
Mental experience (following thoughts)	Bodily experience (witnessing breath)
Self-study and learning	Self-practice and being
Contemplating, reflecting on the moment	Appreciating and absorbing the moment
Identifying emotions	Feeling sensations
You might find your eyes roll upward (thinking)	Your eyes are soft and likely to be looking downward

The space between the subtle transition from self-reflection to self-awareness is important for you to notice because often this is the space where the voice of your ego can slip in. It is your ego that gets you to lick your wounds and focus on your hurt, fear, and pain. Your soul, on the other hand, is what allows you to relish in your strengths, appreciate the healing that is taking place, and accept the wisdom being delivered. The looking inward process is about bridging that gap, standing up to your inner bully (ego), and letting yourself feel the quiver while allowing yourself to receive the blessing of your raw emotions.

Here is the thing: it is because you have great promise that you are being challenged. This is the mindset I had to develop to look inward (self-reflect) without spiraling back into reactivity. Here is an example of how this can occur.

At one point during my healing journey, I had a rough weekend. My husband and I had gone out and were surrounded by people we had known for years. Until then, he and I hadn't been very social, as we were rebuilding our relationship. I knew at some point I would have to reintegrate into the social scene, but what I didn't expect was how overwhelmingly sensitive I would be to the process. I felt disconnected, and as I stayed in my seat, I engaged in self-reflection. I noticed my thoughts and actions and observed that I was like an adolescent who can be overly sensitive to every movement and look. The experience left me drained and unable to make the transition into self-awareness. I succumbed to the voice of my ego, which reminded me how hurt and damaged I was.

The next day, things were still bad and I thought I might need medication. I felt I had no business writing a book because if I couldn't help myself, then how in the world could I help someone else? That's when I realized I needed to challenge those negative thoughts and stand up to the inner bully of my ego.

RESETTING YOUR NERVOUS SYSTEM

What I didn't know at the time was that what can happen in this gap between self-reflection and self-awareness is you can retraumatize yourself. You can feel symptoms similar to those you experienced during a former event or circumstance in your life. As a result, you revisit similar thoughts, and in many cases that means the *what ifs*. It can be as simple as remembering a time when you received some really bad news.

This is how the Look Inward step came to be. I had read some of the work of Peter A. Levine, PhD, about how people who experience a physical and emotional trauma begin to shake and tremor. In his book *In an Unspoken Voice: How the Body Releases Trauma and Restores Goodness*, Levine discusses how medical response teams are quick to stop the shaking of trauma victims by giving them a shot of Valium or by holding them down. He says this increases the chances they will later experience post-traumatic stress disorder (PTSD). The shaking and trembling, according to Levine, are how the body is attempting to reset the nervous system, decreasing the chances that a person will have PTSD.

YOUR LOOKING INWARD STATEMENT

The ego cannot survive in self-awareness. This is because the ego feeds on thoughts. If you are someone who has a tendency to want to talk about and label your emotions, this can be a roundabout way of thinking. There are times (like when you are communicating with someone) when self-reflection is helpful, such as if you are expressing how you feel. However, this second C.L.E.A.N.S.E. step is focused on self-awareness to dissolve the ego and allow (rather than stop) your nervous system's reset.

When my inner voice (ego) said, "I look like a fool," I could move from self-reflection to self-awareness by saying, "How I feel in my body right now is jittery, tight, alert," which is an example of a looking inward statement.

Here are some questions to help you write your own looking inward statement:

- What is your inner voice telling you?
- In this moment, how do you feel in your body? List the sensations (e.g., heavy, warm, cool, tight, tense, open, pressure).

THE BOOBY TRAP

After listing your sensations, don't linger there or you'll fall into what I refer to as a "booby trap." Notice your sensations, but do not dwell on them. Think of it like a toddler who may wander away. Your mind, without discipline and redirection, will do the same. Step 2 (Look Inward) slows your brain down, which is why you trail off into thought. The thoughts are one of the ways your subconscious mind controls discomfort. I'll give you other tools for relief in Step 7 (Ease).

After an uncomfortable social event, I would revisit what had occurred by quietly moving through the C.L.E.A.N.S.E. formula, beginning with Step 1 (Clear) and noticing what I was feeling in my body. I observed how the negative sensations were connected to the memory of the event. This is the thing about sensations: you don't have to be experiencing the actual event to clear the reactivity and digest the raw emotions.

Take a moment to try this:

- Sit in a chair and straighten up your body.

- Place your feet flat on the floor about hip-width apart. Sit with intention, as if you are going to make a statement.

- Visualize your strong, alert spine bearing against the thoughts that tell you to resist, give up, or hold back.

- Without moving your head or shoulders, gaze down at the floor. Acknowledge that you are making a decision to transition from self-reflection to self-awareness.

- Breathe and notice!

How I feel in my body right now is _____ .

SETTLING INTO SELF-AWARENESS

Now that you have placed your attention on your sensations, you can begin to settle into your self-awareness. This means focusing on your breathing. Focused breathing strengthens your ability to move from self-reflection into self-awareness.

MAKING THE MOST OF YOUR EXHALE

Settling into your body usually happens on the exhale. It's like what sighing a loud sigh feels like at the end of a long day. Your exhale signals to your body that you are choosing to give yourself a break, relax, and recalibrate.

The way in which you exhale, however, makes a difference. Short, quick, and premature exhales are likely to leave incomplete, unresolved emotions within you. On the other hand, a long, slow, mindful exhale creates a stronger movement of energy (emotions), giving you the means to release reactivity. As you learn to look inward and move into a long exhale, observe the ways in which reactivity has been housed in your body through both conscious and unconscious patterns.

Exhaling from your chest (squeezing your heart) does not move (digest) your emotions. It isn't until you practice learning how to pull in your navel from your lower abdomen that you will be able to truly settle in. The easiest way to learn this is by lying down on your back and pulling in your lower abdomen on the exhale to the count of three (exhale 1, 2, 3). Once you get the hang of it lying down, you can practice it sitting or standing up tall with your feet firmly planted on the floor (hip-width apart).

When you pull in your navel (toward your spine) on the exhale, you are accessing the lower lobes of your lungs. This is where calming nerves are found. Your exhale also helps you to release carbon dioxide from your bloodstream. This gives your body a chance to release gases and acidity. Stress, environmental pollutants, and overprocessed foods cause acidity. When your body does not release carbon dioxide efficiently, this clogs the pathway from bringing in fresh oxygen to your heart, which is the central station for pumping out blood to the rest of the organs. It will be difficult for you to both notice (self-awareness) and feel these benefits if you are not exhaling properly.

Keep in mind that the intention of your exhale in this section is to help you settle into your state of awareness. The more you practice this, the less you will get distracted and pull yourself out of these states. It is possible to be present and aware most of the time. It is a simple shift of your awareness. To support the process, move your gaze (eyes) from looking upward (which usually means you are engaging in thought) to glancing downward when you exhale. Also keep your feet flat on the floor and your shoulders back and down. These actions will help you develop your ability to be present and aware.

INHALING SAFETY

Breathing more slowly and deeply lowers your blood pressure, increasing your healing capacities. You know your inhale is deep when the muscles between your ribs widen and your diaphragm moves down. This is easiest when you are sitting up tall with your shoulders back and down. Think of your inhale as inflating a tire tube; with each breath it increases the volume. Once again, breathing through your nose and if necessary counting on the inhale (1, 2, 3...) will help you develop a strong inhale.

Your inhale is what prepares you for a transition. Whether it be a physical transition (seated to standing) or a transition between C.L.E.A.N.S.E. steps, your inhales give you energy. This keeps you motivated and alert. Each time you inhale, you take in oxygen. Oxygen helps you burn the fuel in your body (sugar, fatty acids, and emotions). The more energy you have, the less this process will seem like a chore. As you circulate oxygen, reactivity continues to decrease while your ability to feel (without judgment) increases. This is because when the body is receiving oxygen and releasing carbon dioxide efficiently, it feels safe.

How you inhale makes a difference. Ideally it is helpful if you can create an evenness in your breathing. You might inhale to the count of three and exhale to the count of three. If you overinhale, you can sometimes stimulate the fight-or-flight response. You will know this because you will feel a little nervous or light-headed or you might have trouble thinking. Your body needs an even exchange of inhaling and exhaling to fully settle into self-awareness.

What I have found is many people have trained their exhales to react as a protective mechanism. You might feel tension in a room and notice how your body begins to hold back its breath and tighten up its solar plexus (navel) area. When you react to tension in this way, it feels as if you have wrapped a tourniquet around your midsection—blood, oxygen, and energy get cut off. If this continues, you are likely to feel disconnected, unsure, and unsafe.

According to Bessel van der Kolk, MD, in *The Body Keeps the Score*, "Many traumatized people find themselves chronically out of sync with the people around them." For years, I felt like I did not fit in. When I was younger, my brother killed two people while driving under the influence of drugs and alcohol, and from that point on it would take me years before I was able to fully inhale and exhale again. In many ways, living with an affair felt all too familiar; I could never let my guard down and show my true pain.

Feeling safe is a nontoxic state. This is a state where you can learn, grow, heal, and trust. It is when your body feels unharmed that it will allow you to explore and release deeper levels of trauma. You cannot get to that level through talking alone. By only talking through your trauma, you risk staying put in self-reflection. To fully look inward, you must be able to cross the bridge into self-awareness. Then from there you can begin body dialoging.

BODY DIALOGING

Body dialoging is the process of speaking directly to your body and listening for feedback via observation. This is different from when you speak to another person. When you speak to other people, you are often noticing their nonverbal body language and hearing their words for feedback. When it comes to your body, you are noticing sensations—*dull, sharp, warm, cool, tight, heavy, light, or clogged.*

It was through the process of body dialoguing that I could fully digest the onslaught of triggers I received after the affair. If I followed the triggers—meaning if I began to think about and analyze things—this only led to reactive behaviors such as ranting and raving, maybe not to the other person directly but aloud. I might articulate my thoughts while driving in my car, groaning about what I would say or how I felt about a certain situation or person. Body dialoging means you begin a conversation with your body through the looking inward statement:

How I feel in my body right now is _____.

What I realized was that many of my triggers were in place long before my marriage—they were rooted in my childhood.

At a conference for social workers I asked my standard question: "Who in this room thinks they are the most stressed?" A few hands went up, and I asked one of the participants how she knew this.

"Because I am always tense in my neck and shoulders."

I then asked her why this was.

She replied, "I had an accident a couple of years ago."

"Why don't we ask your body?" I suggested.

The woman sat upright in a chair, with her feet flat on the floor. I asked her to close her eyes and then said, "Body, are you available to tell us why her shoulders and neck are so tense?" I repeated this two or three times, paused, and guided her to take a deep inhale and exhale through her nose (focusing on the sensations she was experiencing).

I asked the woman if her body gave her any responses.

"I don't think so, but I feel less pain."

At the end of the conference she ran over to me happily and said, "My neck and shoulders are completely pain free! Thank you!"

Developing a healthy communication is a two-way street. It means learning the skills of both asking and receiving. This is how you will handle this process; you will practice asking and receiving the feedback. Notice I say *feedback* rather than *answers*. This is because I have found many people have a fear of feedback. They cringe at the thought of displeasing someone else. The reason is that somewhere along the line they trained themselves to be a people-pleaser or to fear embarrassment. If this resonates for you, know that it is an unhealed part of your past. Opening the dialogue between you and your body will help heal it. It allows this suppressed energy (emotions, beliefs) to be seen and heard and to elevate to the surface for healing. The purpose of looking inward is to allow old, unhealed wounds to become evident, as you will be emitting (transforming) them in Step 3.

SHAPING YOUR INTENTIONS

The looking inward process shapes your intentions. When you speak your intentions without first tuning into your body, they become man-made from the brain. Intentions evolve naturally when they are shaped by focusing on how you are showing up in your body.

I can't tell you how many times I showed up to therapy thinking I was going to work on a specific issue with my husband, and then as I inhaled and exhaled into my body, the intentions of our session would shift. This was true with the C.L.E.A.N.S.E. formula as well. I'd sit down and think, "I better release this fear," but as I entered the steps, I would find myself embracing my whole emotions. What I learned was *fear is not a whole emotion*, it is a reaction, and the only thing to embody after that is love.

When we live primarily from the brain, our nervous system can go into defensive mode. This is how behaviors such as blame and shaming come to be. By noticing how you are showing up (sensation-wise), what you learn is to take responsibility for the energy in your body right now. Outside influences and histories easily distract the brain. As you practice the skill of looking inward through body dialoguing, you will become less influenced by these distractions. You will learn to notice resistance rather than react to it. As this occurs your body softens, and your true self (wholeness) begins to emerge. It is not about he, she, them, this, or those—that is all reactivity. It is only through your whole emotions that you will be able to recognize connection, love, and compassion.

HARMONY

Read this statement aloud: *How I feel in my body right now promotes harmony*. Because you are not offering a label, explanation, or answer, you are training your body to feel rather than react to what is happening in the moment. Here is the thing: you don't have to rehash the past or predict the future—when you blame your experiences, even the little things like "My hair looks awful today because I didn't wash it" push back the energy of your emotions, and you never get to experience their rawness.

RECAP

- Allow your body to shape your intentions through your "How do I feel in my body right now?" statement.
- Practice bridging the gap between self-reflection and self-awareness, applying bodily awareness and nonjudgment through body dialoging.
- Know that feedback comes in the form of sensations.
- Be mindful not to linger; instead allow your inhale to prepare you for the transition to Step 3.

CLEANSING TIP: INHALE SAFETY, EXHALE SETTLED IN

Practice this mantra while breathing through your nose. Mantras work best when they are spoken aloud and repeated several times in a row. It will look something like this: inhale through your nose; state aloud at the top of your inhale, "Inhale safety"; then exhale; and at the bottom of your exhale (navel in toward spine) say aloud, "Exhale settled in." Do this five times in a row, and at the end say aloud, "Thank you" to your body.

C.L.E.A.N.S.E. STEP 3: EMIT

"He calmed the storm to a whisper and stilled the waves."

—Psalm 107:29

As you read these words, your body is working to eliminate what it does not need. It does this automatically through the functioning of your major organs, such as the kidneys, liver, and skin (sweat glands). Each cell with its own task—working hard, exchanging information, deciding how and when you are ready to release waste. Everything you ingest gets broken down in one form or another, not just food but also your thoughts. Each becomes liquefied into forms of energy. The challenge is that negative or harmful thoughts tend to be lower in vibration. This makes them heavier (like a plate of pasta) and more difficult to digest. However, as with ingesting and digesting your food, the more you relax, pause, and appreciate the process, the easier your thoughts will flow through.

So far in your C.L.E.A.N.S.E., you have asked your body questions and practiced receiving the feedback, and you are now focused on allowing emotional release. Step 3 redirects and releases emotional energy by increasing your engagement with the present moment. One way it does this is through an ancient technique: using sound. Not only does engaging the sound of your own voice release fear but it also puts into place internal boundaries. Here you will learn how energetic boundaries are essential to your overall well-being.

MOVING FROM FEAR TO LOVE

The emission process is not about getting rid of reactivity but instead transforming it into something new, the way manure nourishes crops. After working with hundreds of clients and thousands of students, I've learned the soul does not want to contribute fear to the world; it wants to share, connect, and grow through love.

The Emit step redirects awareness to the present moment, where energy can be transformed from fear to love.

TRANSFORMING ENERGY

You were born from a womb. It doesn't matter whether you are male or female or whether you were raised by your biological or adoptive caregivers or wolves for that matter—your life began inside a womb. You cannot deny that, in every human being, there is something sacred about the energy centers that lie beneath the navel where the reproductive and digestive organs are located. Through connection to these energy centers, the Emit step allows you to release reactivity that has been held over long periods of time. These energy centers are also referred to as the root chakra, sacral chakra, and solar plexus chakra. If you have practiced yoga, you may have heard references to the seven energy centers. Know there are far more than seven. In this section, we will focus on the lower three (genital area; reproductive organs; and solar plexus, which is slightly above the navel).

Chakras are referred to as wheels of life (where energy pools). They contain a natural rhythm of movement. When this movement is in balance, there are many noteworthy benefits. The greatest by far are increased emotional well-being, balance, harmony, and improved organ and immune system function. These benefits happen because balancing out your chakras (which you will do using some of the suggestions in this step) is a way to digest your emotions, including the ones that have been frozen over time due to trauma.

You can't necessarily see chakras (wheels of energy in motion); however, through ancient practices such as yoga, Reiki, tai chi, acupuncture, chanting, prayer, and meditation, you can certainly feel them. Chakras, when in balance, tend to move in a clockwise direction with a noticeable amount of feeling. On the other hand, when they are out of balance, they might move counterclockwise. This makes them feel dull, lifeless, and dense. Chakras can become imbalanced by spinning too fast and wide, and as a result you may feel out of sorts, distracted, and anxious or experience extreme mood swings. Individuals trained in healing modalities such as massage or Reiki can hover their hands (with fingers closed) close to the body and feel these molecules and atoms in motion.

During the Emit step, you are tuning into these centers (through your awareness) and employing practices that both transform and balance your energy (emotions). Without this piece, you may temporarily feel relief by being relaxed and present; however, this doesn't mean you have changed the energy pattern. Think of energy patterns as predictable rhythms of movement. Anger, for example, has a predictable amount of movement and intensity in the body, which is how you can identify it. This is why it is important to practice the C.L.E.A.N.S.E. formula regularly (daily, if possible), because over time you will change these patterns.

SOUND WAVES

If you listen to someone playing an acoustic guitar, each time a chord is struck, a sound wave travels through your body. This is also true when you listen to your voice sing a tune. Certain sounds have healing capacities. As I wrote in *Choosing Love*, scientists have calibrated the vibration of love as 528 hertz, and this vibration is embedded into pieces of music like the Gregorian chants. Using sound is something I recommend for transforming toxicity into bliss. It is simple, accessible, and free. The best part is, it is your energy. There is nothing synthetic about it. You being you and me being me is what makes this process so effective and profound.

According to Margaret Rouse, "A sound wave is the pattern of disturbance caused by the movement of energy traveling through a medium (such as air, water, or any other liquid or solid matter)." The key phrase I want to point out is *pattern of disturbance caused by the movement of energy*. As mentioned earlier, patterns are predictable cycles of energy that contribute to the way you think, feel, and act. They also influence overprocessing your emotions. When left undisturbed these patterns can turn into belief systems. Not just within yourself but among communities and cultures.

You may have grown up in a family that constantly repeated, "Money doesn't grow on trees." Without realizing it, this mindset might haunt you today—how you feel about spending money, how many hours you choose to work, and whether you allow yourself to take a vacation. It may also affect the amount of movement (processing) in your emotions. You may not realize it, but each time you hand over a dollar bill or use your credit card, you might get a slight squeezing of your organs, which tells you that you are in reactivity.

Attempting to shift this pattern by changing your thoughts alone can have a positive impact on the relationship between you and money. However, to truly cleanse this reaction (toxicity) to money and receive the energy within the raw emotions, sound is one of your greatest tools. This may be why prayer and mantras (repeated syllables, words, or phrases) are so effective when spoken aloud. Let's begin with some of the natural, innate sounds you have already been using. One is the sound of "ah..." and the other is "mmm..." After a nice, cool shower on a hot day, you may find the "ah..." slips so easily out of your mouth. Likewise with the "mmm..." sound after eating something so yummy. If you allow yourself to sink into these sounds while being in a state of self-awareness, you will begin to feel different. This is because you are changing the energy inside you. When babies are first using language, they instinctually use cooing or babbling sounds. I often wonder if what they are truly illustrating is how we are naturally connected to our raw emotions.

To try it out, I suggest sitting up tall and taking a deep inhale right now, inflating the sides of your waist. On your out breath (exhale) say "ah," pressing your navel toward your spine. Notice how this sound vibrates all the way down your body into your toes. To make the most of this tool, you will simultaneously lift your pelvic floor as you exhale. (You will learn about lifting your pelvic floor in the next section.)

When I reach Step 3, I use the sound "hum," taken from the mantra "So Hum," which is translated as "I am that." After writing *Mantras Made Easy*, I learned how Sanskrit is known to be a highly vibrational language, meaning it creates a lot of movement in the body. "Hum" works for me; however, you can hum a single note instead if you like. The key is to draw out the sound long enough for your navel to pull in and your pelvic floor to lift.

LIFTING YOUR PELVIC FLOOR

Your pelvis is the foundation of your body. When your pelvis is weak, this can lead to lower-back pain and physical instability (creating poor posture). Lifting (squeezing the muscles) in your pelvic floor during exhale creates a strong foundation, making you less susceptible to overprocessing your emotions. It also concentrates the pools of energy of the lower chakras, allowing the sound to penetrate and transform the energy more readily. As this occurs, you will notice a feeling of centeredness and stability begin to surface.

Try it. Take a long inhale (through your nose), and exhale an audible "ah" while lifting the pelvic floor simultaneously. As you lift the pelvic floor (which means you slightly engage or squeeze the muscles you use to go to the bathroom) while making this sound, you are allowing the sound waves to penetrate the pool of energy in the lower chakras (root and sacral). These lower chakras are like little energetic recordings of your energetic history. The root chakra (in the genitals) has been noted to carry your ancestral memories and survival instincts. Once again, you are lifting (squeezing) this area while placing your awareness there. It is the combination of your exhale and lifting the pelvic floor while placing your awareness on these lower energy centers that allows you to increase stability. This makes your body feel protected and safe. Notice this dual action (sound coupled with lifting the pelvic floor) automatically releases your jaw. This is an important part of the emission process, explained as follows.

JAW RELEASE

There is a direct connection between your core (lower energy centers and abdominals) and jaw. If you were to contract your abdominals now, drawing them inward toward the spine, you would notice how your jaw automatically wants to open. It is darn hard to clench your teeth and lift your pelvic floor at the same time. Having a tight jaw is like placing a clamp on your emotional flow, affecting the way you communicate with yourself and others. Your jaw affects your throat energy center (sixth chakra). Your throat can be considered the bridge between your heart and mind. Blocking this bridge through tense, constricted energy is what gets you to speak with reactivity and criticism.

When your throat is affected by heavy, blocked emotional energy, this can impact your thyroid gland (located at the base of your neck), which is responsible for regulating breathing, heart rate, body temperature, metabolism, and more—and each of these things that the thyroid regulates plays a role in the processing of your emotions. As you practice the seven steps, you will notice how your body temporarily heats up or cools itself down during the process. This aids your emotional digestion. Tight jaws can lead to blocked energy in the throat, which can contribute to physical symptoms such as sore throats, neck pain, and headaches.

I wrote earlier about how emotional detoxes help you have a stronger core. This is because not only are you learning how to engage your abdominal muscles (as you exhale and pull your navel toward your spine) and lift your pelvic floor (engaging your buttocks and strengthening your spine), but also, as you release your jaw, the locked energy in your throat is able to circulate, giving your muscles and blood newfound energy. Sure, you can get stronger muscling your way through abdominal crunches; however, when you scrunch up your face and tighten your muscles (jaw), you may be working a lot harder than you ought to. Release your jaw and allow the energy to distribute throughout your entire body, and all your organs and muscles will benefit.

Now that you understand the energetic connection to your physical body, let's get a little deeper into how your physical body is designed to process emotions. Before going there, take a deep breath, inflating your abdomen, and on the exhale, lift your pelvic floor, release your jaw (allowing it to drop open), and say "ah" at the end of your breath. Inhale through your nose, and draw your attention to your lower abdomen and colon.

THE COLON CONNECTION

I was on birth control, and when my children were young, I spent a year trying out five different antidepressants. I suffered intolerable side effects, making it increasingly difficult for me to function. I eventually gave up and started to explore more mindful forms of treatment. Little did I know taking daily prescription drugs had an impact on my gut and colon. I would blame my bloated stomach on having babies and ignore the fact that I was rarely going to the bathroom. What no one told me, as Adam Hadhazy wrote in *Scientific American,* was that "95 percent of the body's serotonin [known to elevate mood and alleviate depression] is found in the bowels." I was blocking my body's ability to produce serotonin!

If you suffer from depression, anxiety, weight gain, moodiness, irritability, skin rashes, or other conditions, you might want to consider creating a lifestyle that supports your gut and colon. Part of the support includes developing an awareness of your breath and relaxing your body so it is more able to flush out the remnants of toxins left from stress, prescription drugs, and other environmental pollutants.

During my healing journey, I went to see a colonics specialist, Pam McDermott. I knew if I was going to heal from this emotional trauma, I had to make sure my pipes were working properly. As she explained the procedure, I lay on her table and started to tell her the real reason I was there. "My husband had an affair," I said. I must confess that not only did I hope to help open the passageway of being able to relieve myself emotionally, I was also looking for ways to feel more cleansed. The affair left me feeling dirty and contaminated.

"Emotions," Pam said, "are processed through the gut." She reiterated the statistic—95 percent of available serotonin is produced and stored in the gut. She talked about how our bowels and brain are constantly exchanging messages.

However, for many of us, the messages travel just one way (from colon to brain); therefore, most messages are being sent upward. This makes it more likely that your gut adjusts your moods (rather than your gut and brain working together). If the gut isn't working properly, these messages will be ones of distress. You will know this because you are feeling bloated, constipated, and irritated.

When it comes to emitting your toxicity, it will be important to make this brain-gut connection. As you lift the pelvic floor and release your jaw through sound, allow this wave (vibration) to travel all the way into your gut and colon. This means you will drop your awareness to these lower chakras. Without dropping your awareness, the vibration is likely to stay concentrated in your chest. The purpose is to tap into these areas (the gut and colon) and give them a little jiggle so that the vibration increases your body's ability to naturally emit what it no longer needs.

SETTING BOUNDARIES

Many of us have been taught that boundaries are like a line in the sand. This is your side, and this is mine. Cross the line, and you are in my territory. Boundaries for many have been a form of control. How you may or may not describe your limits, what you will and will not tolerate. At least this is what it has been like for me. The trouble is that setting boundaries in this way, when done from the throes of reactivity, hampers rather than strengthens relationships.

For most of my life boundaries have been an issue. Either I come on too strong or I become oblivious to having them at all. I might implement them one minute and tear them down the next. This is because I would feel guilty or frustrated with the process. That is until I got to this step (Emit). What this step taught me is that implementing boundaries is not just an act, it is also an experience.

We cannot control other people—we can influence them, but we don't have full control over their words or actions. You will be far more influential if you are clear about knowing and communicating about your boundaries. Otherwise, you risk losing energy maintaining them. You might rant about your mother-in-law and how she oversteps into your relationship. This ranting comes at quite an energetic cost—you leak emotional energy rather than transforming it. You know this is happening when something creates conflict and disconnection within yourself and others.

RELEASING FROM YOUR CORE

The Emit step strengthens your connection to your pelvic floor. As you exhale and gently squeeze your genital muscles (while releasing your jaw and unhinging the back teeth), you are likely to sense a feeling of stability. You will also be engaging your navel and pulling it in and up, like a zipper on a coat. Doing this on a regular basis will strengthen your core!

Incorporating the "ah" sound redirects the energy you stirred in Step 1 to a place where it can be transformed. You will get used to this process and over time begin to recognize your tummy muscles as a source of strength and stability. I find it interesting that the one part of the body that is so capable of transforming fear to love (the abdominals) is the area we tend to pick on the most. We poke at our tummies or pick on our love handles; no wonder we are hesitant to turn to our bodies for an emotional release.

During my emotional detox, there was a part of me that wanted to physically hold onto my husband, to tell him where he could and could not go. I didn't need to, though, because he had already implemented some physical changes. He called me often to tell me where he was and what his plans were. This was a big change for us, as we tended to lead parallel lives, keeping most of the details to ourselves, but now he was instilling his own boundaries while working on rebuilding my trust. This put me at ease, allowing me to focus on my healing.

Another way boundaries and our core are connected is through our speech. I find when we speak or act from our heads, our voices project out through our throats and hearts where reactivity tends to house itself. However, when we speak from our core, our voices are more rooted from our whole emotions. This is because the pelvic floor is engaged, keeping us connected with the present moment, where reactivity does not exist. This cleanses our speech, making it less likely we will be careless.

I encourage my clients to practice speaking from their core. I ask them to pretend their navel is their mouth. Then I have them engage their midsection while they talk. This forces the tone of their voice to deepen; they often report needing to say fewer words and feeling more assertive and grounded.

Try it!

- Take a deep inhale.
- Sit up tall and begin to command your body.
- You have already come so far. You know how to tone down reactivity, and you are willing to look inward and ask questions, so now draw your navel in, lift your pelvis, and as you release your jaw, allow the sound of "ah" to penetrate your lower belly; while doing so, make a conscious connection to your colon.

- Feel your legs, feet, and toes receiving the energy.

- Notice how this energy rebuilds your root system. Your root system is the foundation for your core values. Nurture them with your breath and they will grow stronger.

Know you will be far more effective at setting and respecting boundaries for yourself and others as you develop this skill.

RECAP

- Emit means you are redirecting your awareness to the present moment through sound.

- Chanting "hum" or "ah" or simply humming vibrates in the lower lobes of your lungs when you lift your pelvic floor, creating a sense of safety, stability, and strength, which is essential before transitioning into Step 4.

CLEANSING TIP: HEART VISUALIZATION

Imagine your heart is your eyes. Just as you soften your eyes into a gaze, soften your heart. Allow it to melt and gradually diffuse itself. Softened hearts are vulnerable and weepy. Allow the tears to flow from this space. Just as you might squint your eyes and squeeze your face during a good hard cry, allow this experience to come from your heart center. Breathe, surrender, and soften.

C.L.E.A.N.S.E. STEP 4: ACTIVATE JOY

*"Jesus said, 'Ask and you will receive, and
your joy will be complete.'"*

—John 16:24

When a battery is losing its power, some of the signs are its case is leaking, bloating, and swelling. If you were to remove an old car battery and replace it with a new one, your vehicle would run better. It might also bring you a renewed faith in your car. Rather than seeing it as old and unreliable, you might be content with keeping it around longer. Activating joy is similar. When it is leaking, life becomes robotic. You are going through the motions; however, the progress you are making may seem arduous and sluggish.

Activations are about expansion. Think of them like a kick-start. When you learn to ride a bike, you might need a little push; likewise, your energy might need a little nudge outward. To do this, you need to be aware of what you can't see—the power of your aura—as well as practical concerns like the difference between wanting and having and joy versus happiness.

Here is the thing: activations open us to what is already here! Everything we desire already exists, including our connection to joy. *Hurrah!*

WHAT YOU CANNOT SEE

On a cloudy day, you might not be able to see the sun, yet you still know it exists. This is the same for joy. Occasionally we get a physical sensation of joy—like when we take a bath or pet a dog—and we get a nonphysical sensation of joy when we see sunlight coming through our window or remember a happy moment. Joy is both a physical and nonphysical experience.

There are many things that exist that we can't see. Think about molecules and atoms. These are the tiny particles that make up both the physical world (e.g., a table) and nonphysical world (the chemical processes of our emotions and thoughts). Since an emotional detox is about cleansing reactivity and embracing our whole emotions, we are transforming ourselves from the molecular level. When it comes to activating, you are tapping into this invisible yet real world of energy.

THIRD EYE AND HEART OPENING

Step 4 begins by activating joy. This guides us as we open our hearts and the space between the eyes, which yogis refer to as our third eye and which is also called ajna chakra (energy center). It is said that if the third eye is blocked (energetically), it leads to confusion, jealousy, and more. However, when it is open, we experience clarity, concentration, intuition, and bliss. Here's how to open your third eye:

1. As you inhale, simultaneously draw your attention to your third-eye center.

2. Take a moment to notice how, when you place your attention on your third eye, the sensation there becomes intensified.

The same sensation would happen if you focused on your right big toe for thirty seconds. Try it. *Cool, right?* Now follow the steps for activating joy:

1. Place your awareness on your heart center until you feel sensation.

2. Shift that awareness to your third eye and feel sensation.

3. Close your eyes and direct all your energy toward joy.

Keep in mind joy is not always physical, so if you need to make this a more concrete experience, visualize a beautiful sunrise or imagine smelling a rose. As you become adept at this process, it won't take long and you'll strengthen your ability to rest in joy.

I often see clients who have had their heart broken. Perhaps they've lost a loved one or a former relationship. They take the time to find their center again; however, something inside them makes them terrified to be in another relationship. Much of this is due to overprocessed emotions, but also at some point they need to relearn how to activate joy.

AURA

Auras are electromagnetic fields that radiate from all things and creatures—humans, plants, animals, bodies of water, and even inanimate objects. Your aura is like a giant magnetic mirror. It reflects what is happening inside you and (like a magnet) attracts what you focus on. If you are irritable, nervous, or insecure, your aura will reflect low or blocked energy. Using Kirlian photography, auras can be photographed; low or blocked energy will show up as heavy or dark colors. Since joy is within us (experienced as a feeling) and around us (a vibrational frequency found in nature), setting it into motion requires a minor shift in attention.

The field of energy around our hearts happens to be sixty times stronger than the one around the brain. Therefore, we cannot think our way to joy; we must feel it. The heart has a wonderful way of both activating joy and cleansing reactivity. If you have ever had a *heartfelt* moment, you will notice how your heart feels light and open (joy), as well as how a good hard cry can cleanse (move) the heaviness around the heart. Joy can be brought to us, and it can come through us. It is a two-way street. The best part is, the more you focus on joy, the stronger your aura will be—and since your aura protects you from and filters out negativity, it will be key to helping you heal (cleanse) and manifest the life you desire.

Once I connected to joy, something cool happened. I started to feel a deep sense of appreciation—not just for the progress my husband and I were making but also for the simple things. A smile of a stranger, a bird outside my window, and the sun on my face. Sure, I had felt these feelings before, but this time was different, or perhaps I was different. Then something made me realize joy was within me; I stopped wanting and started becoming interested in living.

What I realized was that a long time ago, I made a decision to stop living. I traded fun, laughter, and light-heartedness for responsibilities, worries, and obligations. For the first time in quite a while, I felt movement in my heart (like butterflies). No matter what landed in front of me, I was no longer afraid. I could sense goodness (joy) in front of me. I knew it was joy because it didn't feel fake, scripted, or initiated from my brain. I didn't feel the need to talk about it because words could never express what I felt. Being in joy, I felt content and free. Shortly after, I came across this Bible verse from Romans 14:17: "Joy is the natural reaction to the work of God, whether promised or fulfilled. Joy expresses God's kingdom—His influence on earth."

WANTING AND HAVING

To support joy activation, it is important to notice the difference between *wanting* and *having*. The intention is to help you get clear on what exactly you are placing your attention on as you open your third eye and heart center.

WANTING	HAVING
Brain-driven	Heart-driven
Comes from lack or fear	Comes from plenty or love
Has a more sluggish energy	Is rich with energy
Fear-driven (despair)	Love-inspired (hope)
Narrow lens/perception (feels wrong)	Open lens/perception (feels right)

ENCOUNTERING JOY

Although joy and happiness are both pleasurable feelings, they are different. Lifestyle mentor and psychologist Rachel Fearnley says that joy "comes when you make peace with who you are, why you are, and how you are." Happiness happens when you experience pleasure in your surroundings. Sure, you can create happiness by saying something kind to someone else, going out for a nice meal with friends, or putting a beautiful vase of flowers on your kitchen table, and I encourage you to do so; however, this will not activate joy.

One day I discovered joy wasn't anything spectacular. I didn't see any rainbows or wake up instantaneously cured from all the heartache. Joy for me came after a long, hard cry. The day before I had focused on Step 1 (clearing reactivity), Step 2 (looking inward), and Step 3 (emission). The next day, I felt like shit. I need you to know this because it turned out to be a great blessing. What I learned a long time ago is that the only way out is through. This means you must go through your emotions to fully digest them. Sorry there are no shortcuts. This is not to say you will have to have a bad day every time you move through the steps; however, in the beginning, stuff may surface. I will continue the story in a moment, but first...

That's how I encountered joy. I want you to know if you are feeling low, this could be a sign that joy is on its way. The day I felt shitty, I decided to do something different. My heart led me to the backyard of my mother's house. I knew she was away, so I sat at the picnic table in her backyard under the trees with the sun shining on my back. I did what my heart desired: write. I wrote for about two hours. Although the words didn't quite come out right and I erased them later, I would leave that experience feeling renewed. I told my oldest daughter, "Something shifted in my heart—it feels like I had some sort of activation."

When I found out about the affair, I took my wedding rings off. In my mind, the vows were broken, so what was the point? It was also a way to remind myself that I needed time before I made any big decisions. I confess after eighteen years of wearing my rings, this was not easy. A few times I considered putting them back on, but it was too much of a trigger until nine months later. One day after work I went home and took a shower. It was then I started taking in joy, the warmth of the water, the sound of my little ones' footsteps outside my door, and the memory of the beautiful conversation I had with my husband earlier that morning. That's when I started to think about my wedding rings—I had an urge to put them back on. I got out of the shower, rummaged through my drawer, pulled out a little satin bag, and found a note I had forgotten I'd written to myself in the throes of the crisis. It read: "Dear Sheri, no matter what happens, I love you. —God."

It was as if God wanted me to know my sense about an activation was correct. God wanted me to know he or she was with me. But the story does not end there. Later I received a phone call from a dear friend who creates prayer beads. I had paid her to make a set for me. She had picked up a set of beads (thinking they were her own) and started praying. She looked down and realized she had been praying over the beads she had made for me. This all "coincidentally" happened on my birthday, and once again I could feel God's presence.

JOY IS A PURIFIER

This is how I got to know joy as a purifier. As you set your attention on joy, its energetic frequency is capable of cleansing and breaking old patterns. Think of joy as an energetic eraser. Each time you attune your third eye and heart center to joy, you are choosing to erase reactive patterns and bring forth your raw emotions. When we strip joy from life, we have nothing left but pure resistance.

Here's how to distinguish between happiness and joy:

HAPPINESS	JOY
Is a temporary emotion	Is an infinite connection
Etches a moment in time	Erases reactive patterns
Involves experiencing good fortune (like a new job)	Involves experiencing the Divine

HAPPINESS	JOY
Is more of an external experience	Is more of an internal experience
Can be conditional	Is unconditional
Can be altered	Is permanent
Is gleeful	Is peaceful, calming
Ignites	Cleanses
Is a burst of positive energy	Is resiliency
Is invigorating	Is grounding

DESIRE

Bringing joy into your life begins with a calling. A calling is a strong urge to act, move forward, or live your life in a certain way—like I did when I felt the urge to go to my mother's house to write. To call forth joy you must acknowledge your innermost cravings. These are your desires. The word *desire* can be traced back to the Latin phrase *de sidere* ("from the stars"), which comes from the Latin word *sidus* ("heavenly body"), meaning it is of spirit or God source. You cannot desire what you don't already have. The reason you have desire is because it is one of the ways you connect to your most natural state: joy.

If you crave connection, go for a walk and be with connection through nature. If you yearn for love, then be with love—sing, dance, write a letter. If you are hungry for respect, then be with respect. The Persian poet Rumi famously said, "Let yourself be silently drawn by the strange pull of what you really love." This is how you will uncover the joy that is already within you.

If you are not sure what your heart's desire is, you can joggle it by asking yourself a few questions:

- What am I craving?
- What would I do if money weren't an issue?

- What keeps popping up in my mind as something I might enjoy or am drawn to?
- What opens my heart?
- What soothed me or interested me when I was a child?
- What does my intuition nudge me to do?

Keep in mind, joy is not something you have to figure out. As a creative being, you already have joy within you. *A Course in Miracles* states that "joy and peace are my inheritance." Seeing joy as something that has already been given to you is a life changer. No longer do you have to waste energy seeking, wanting, and hoping for joy, because your creator has already given it. Activating joy is not something you do but is instead a natural desire to be close to that which you love.

MAKING YOUR SELECTION

The Emit step has allowed you to feel grounded. The reactivity in your body is reduced (via Steps 1, 2, and 3), and your energy is beginning to transform (Step 4). You are aware of your nudge, your inner itch that moves you toward desire. Selecting joy is allowing your energy to flow through your heart and third-eye center. To strengthen your connection, soften your eyes into a gaze. This will deepen your breathing. When you stare outward through your eyes when they are fully open, your energy tightens, meaning it has less room to grow. Go ahead and try. Open your eyes wide and stare across the room. Notice how your breathing elevates into your chest and tension seeps into your shoulders. This means your heart feels startled and protective, like a frightened cat. Now soften your eyes into a gaze by looking at the floor with your eyes (keeping your chin parallel to the floor) while connecting to your core, which was activated in the Emit step. Again, you want to feel grounded and secure in the lower half of your body. Now, as if you had an actual eyeball between your brows, allow that area of energy to expand out like a laser beam while softening your eyes. Notice how your heart feels more relaxed and open (less startled). Your energy feels safe exploring and scanning your aura and will, therefore, be more likely to select (pull back) energies that match it (joy).

You will notice in the process just described that you are not speaking. This is because activating your heart and third eye happens from silence. You will not be speaking in Step 4. If you find yourself speaking aloud to yourself or someone else about what you want to do someday, then take a moment, close your eyes, and breathe into your heart space. Open your third eye (while closing your eyes), widen your lens, and let your heart lead the way. You might be pleasantly surprised by what comes back to you—perhaps some insight, a gentle nudge, a reminder to take a certain class, or bumping into someone who can support you on your journey.

When I listened in the shower and heard the voice of my higher self as it encouraged me to put my rings back on, what I didn't realize at the time was that I desired quiet. That is what led me to write at my mother's house. As I zoomed out into my field (aura), opening my heart and third eye, joy was drawn back into my heart. I knew it because I wanted to take full responsibility for what I was feeling. I felt propelled to apologize to anyone I had hurt, make amends with those who were affected by my reactions, and let all people I encountered know how beautiful and special they are. This is what life looks like when you activate joy.

ONENESS

Our next step is to attune ourselves to joy's energy. This means allowing ourselves to connect to its presence. One of the greatest things about joy is it is always present—in that beautiful sunrise I mentioned earlier or a special tree you enjoy visiting. The trouble is, we see ourselves as separate from that sunrise even though we are made of the same thing.

It is when you recognize that same beautiful flower in front of you exists inside of you that joy will become more palpable. You and that flower are essentially one. The flower is in you and you are in that flower. This is what it is like to live in joy. Once you make this shift, you realize how abundant this frequency of joy is, how much our creator must love us to give us all this joy on Earth.

Now back to vulnerability. One of the most effective ways to adjust your energy permanently to joy is to allow yourself to experience vulnerability. According to Brené Brown, PhD, in *Daring Greatly*, "Once we make the connection between vulnerability and joy, the answer is pretty straightforward: We're trying to beat vulnerability to the punch. We don't want to be blindsided by hurt." Through my healing journey, I learned vulnerability is key to accepting yourself and others for who they are, rather than whom you might prefer them to be.

It was by a poolside on a short trip away from home that my daughter befriended a little girl; the girl's mother, who I was sitting next to, asked me about my books on anxiety, which led to the disclosure of her husband's betrayal. Being out of town put me at ease, and with that I could share my experience. Although her situation had occurred years before mine, the hurt and nervousness were still visible. She was contemplating whether or not she should stay with her husband. I asked her if she loved him and if she thought he loved her. Her response was "I feel better when he is not around." And as far as him loving her, she wasn't sure. That is when she turned to me and said, "How can you be so sure your husband loves you?" My response was "Because I can feel it."

One of the most natural ways to access vulnerability is by gazing into your own eyes or the eyes of another. The eyes are the gateway to your soul. If you were to look in a mirror and speak directly to yourself (while looking directly in your eyes), you would feel the rawness of your emotions. It would be through months of couples therapy that my husband and I would be positioned in two straight-back chairs, only a few inches apart, looking directly into each other's eyes. Words didn't even need to be exchanged. The tears streaming down our faces spoke volumes. Nothing is more raw and vulnerable than that. What I know now, which I didn't know then, is that joy was simultaneously being downloaded into my psyche, as well as my emotional fabric, and was soon to be the foundation of our relationship.

RECAP

- Activate joy by placing your attention on your third eye and heart center.
- Breathe into joy.
- If you need to make joy concrete, visualize nature.
- See joy as a powerful cleanser.
- Understand the difference between wanting and having.
- Notice the gentle nudges that call forth joy in your life. *What do you desire?*
- Attune yourself to joy through vulnerability.

CLEANSING TIP: REPLACE YOUR BATTERIES

In this exercise, you will take your dominant hand and, with closed fingers and your palm facing your body, make counterclockwise (and then clockwise) circles up and down the front of your body (a couple of inches away from it). You can do this exercise standing up or sitting up tall in a chair. The idea is that you move your hand a couple of inches in front of the seven energy centers (referred to as chakras), where energy gets pooled. Begin at the base in front of the pubic bone and then move two inches below the navel, two inches above the navel, in front of your heart, in front of your throat, between your eyebrows, and finally at the crown of your head. You will do this twice; the first time, make counterclockwise circles and imagine your hand taking out old, bloated batteries. The second time, switch and move clockwise (with the same hand), and imagine putting in fresh, new batteries. You will be softening your gaze and breathing (inhaling and exhaling) while you go through these motions. At the end, take three deep breaths.

C.L.E.A.N.S.E. STEP 5: NOURISH

"I am not what has happened to me. I am what I choose to become."

—Carl Gustav Jung

To nourish means to sustain, cherish, or keep alive. You might be accustomed to thinking of nourishment as food, the way in which you care for and feed your body. During an emotional detox, "nourish" refers to how you cultivate and respond to your relationships. Rather than with food, you will nourish your relationships with connection, insight, and new skills. Some of these skills include learning how to appreciate others, communicating your *feelings* (rather than thoughts), strengthening your core voice, redefining independence, expressing your needs, noticing the good in others, and granting forgiveness.

Think of those people who might go to a detox program for addiction and make great progress, but when they go out in the real world where everyone knows their history, they begin to fall apart. An emotional detox is similar. Like it or not, some people are going to expect you to react. They might even test you. Not only that but your body (energy) may be expecting you to react. This is because it hasn't been trained otherwise. Once you raise energy by digesting your emotions and choosing joy, the next step is to introduce your body and brain to new ways of handling things. This keeps you from resorting to old ways.

As far as the C.L.E.A.N.S.E. formula is concerned, you will nourish your relationships with an appreciation. Remember, these seven steps will become a three- to five-minute daily practice. When it comes to the nourishing part, you will always offer some sort of an appreciation. I'll go into more detail later, but for now remember you are not actually speaking to a person; you are saying the appreciation aloud as you might recite a prayer or affirmation. One of the reasons this step falls into the formula now is because the next step is Surrender, and to surrender fear, you must connect to the energy of love. Appreciations do that. They strike the core of your emotions, reducing reactivity while circulating your whole emotions.

APPRECIATIONS

My husband and I learned the value of giving appreciations from our Imago therapist Joanne, who trained directly with Harville Hendrix, the founder of Imago therapy. We were taught to give and receive appreciations daily to tone down defensiveness and feel safe. My husband and I were diligent about this. Our appreciations would range anywhere from "I appreciate you taking out the garbage" to "I appreciate the way you love our children."

I took these appreciations beyond our relationship, integrating them into the Nourish phase during my morning meditation. I would select the person or thing that weighed heaviest on my mind, like feeling worried about one of my daughters or hurt by a friend. After I activated joy, I would say aloud, while sitting in my chair, "What I appreciate about _____ (e.g., my daughter) is _____ (e.g., her work ethic)." As soon as I spoke an appreciation statement aloud, I noticed my body would instantly respond by taking a big inhale. As I exhaled, I imagined sending this appreciation off into the world. It felt healing to notice the good in others, and it made sense that this too would be part of the formula.

You will begin to get to know this practice and how it can be applied to any situation. Imago therapy teaches that if anyone is feeling defensive, nobody feels safe, and this disrupts our ability to connect. Here are some other ways you can use appreciations to help reduce reactivity:

REACTION	NOURISH
When you hear yourself thinking negative thoughts about your appearance, say:	"What I appreciate about my body is…"
When you feel unsatisfied or stuck in your work, say:	"What I appreciate about my job is…"
When you think someone does not like you, say:	"What I appreciate about that person is…"
When you are worried about finances, say:	"What I appreciate about money is…"

Once you get the hang of using appreciations to lift your energy and create a safe environment, there are other ways to expand upon the Nourish step, such as strengthening your communication skills. Know that using appreciations is a way to integrate the formula into your daily life. It is like taking yoga off the mat. While on the mat, you are breathing, inhaling, and exhaling, moving into states of connection and disconnection. Use appreciations to bring connection into your life during moments of disconnection (e.g., fear or worry).

GAZE

When practicing yoga, students are encouraged to develop what is referred to as a *drishti* (focused gaze). This is a technique for softening your eyes and setting your gaze in a certain way. It is taught in many different meditation practices. Students might be encouraged to set their gaze on a candle while breathing in and out through their nose. This helps focus their attention while providing a deep inward experience. Now that you have activated joy by opening your third eye and heart center, it's time to nourish by directing that joyful energy inward. Developing your drishti is one way to do this. You don't need to be a yogi to practice this. It is a technique used in many different modalities, including communication building exercises.

When my husband and I first entered therapy, all we had to do was gaze into each other's eyes, and tears would stream down our faces. We didn't need to say a word. When we are in pain, it is so easy to look away and avoid another person's gaze because we are so invested in protecting our pain. I want you to know you don't always have to talk about your pain to heal it, *but you do need to feel it.* Working with gaze brings up so much for people—it opens a window to the soul. If you find someone is avoiding having conversations with you or is withdrawing from a relationship, consider nourishing your connection through meaningful eye contact.

Before doing this, it is important that you let go of any agenda. You might think, "I am going to gaze into my daughter's eyes to get her to open up" or "I am going to make eye contact so my partner will face his challenges." These are agendas, and believe me, the person you are attempting to "fix" will sniff you out.

Here is the difference between having an agenda and being genuine:

AGENDA	GENUINE
Focuses on what you will get or achieve	Focuses on being in a state of connection
Problem-focused	Connection-focused
Concentrates on the past and future	Concentrates on the now
May have a desired outcome in mind	Open to listening

Becoming more intention focused was essential to rebuilding the relationship with my husband. This is not to say I didn't discuss things on our calendar with him, like who would pick up one of the kids when and where. However, when it came to us and our relationship, being genuine was far more effective at creating a healthy dialogue than having an agenda. Having an agenda puts someone in a "damned if they do, damned if they don't" position. You have already decided how things ought to go. However, being genuine and setting aside agendas is difficult to do without first noticing your body.

COMMUNICATION

To be truly nourished in relationship with ourselves and others, healthy communication is essential. This is more than what you will and will not say. Healthy communication is also a way to pay attention to what is happening both inside and outside of your body. It is your ability to nourish that which you are creating, such as love, connection, and happiness.

When you were born, you didn't have any words, so the way you communicated was through sensing and feeling energy. You learned early on to notice the difference between discomfort and comfort. If you had a caregiver who picked you up the moment you cried (like I did with my first daughter), you might have learned that feeling discomfort was bad. As a result, you might have grown up thinking that when grownups were in discomfort (experiencing reactivity), things were not good, so unconsciously you might have given them some of your energy to make them feel better.

At first, this might seem like a good, loving thing to do; however, what I have found is many of these unconscious patterns create wear and tear on your heart, not just emotionally but physically. This is because you have learned how to manage discomfort (whether it be your own or that of others) by protecting (holding back energy from your heart) or trying to make things better (giving away energy from your heart). One of the ways we manage discomfort is by avoiding eye contact.

The challenge is your body doesn't function in separate pieces, meaning what affects your heart also influences other parts of your body, such as your throat. Energetically, your throat is the area for communication. When the energy in this area is clogged, your communication is more likely to be defensive, offensive, or nonexistent. Clients may admit that when things get tense between themselves and another, they either bark back or hold back their true feelings. As I move them through the process, they can see it is their clogged throat, not necessarily their higher (wiser) self, that prevents them from getting out of this negative pattern.

It isn't until we truly listen to our bodies that we will be able to shift such tendencies. Part of that means learning how to become a better listener when you notice your body is in a state of reactivity and to calm it down first. This is why it is important to practice all the C.L.E.A.N.S.E. steps daily. In this step, you are nourishing yourself and others through the art of listening.

BECOMING A LISTENER

Communication can be either beneficial or toxic. This is the way you will think about listening when it comes to your emotional detox. You will release reactivity, and as with a good physical cleanse, you will need to be mindful of the quality of energy you put back in. Like local produce means fresher, better fruits and vegetables, truly listening to others means better communication. Think of it this way: when you buy an apple in the supermarket, that apple may already be days old. This makes it less nutritious. When it comes to an emotional detox, instead of high-quality, nourishing produce, you are looking for high-quality, nourishing dialogue.

I had no idea how nourishing listening could be until I committed to the practice. In the past, I was distracted by my thoughts. I would often put more attention on preparing my response than listening to others. Rebuilding my marriage taught me how true listening fosters connection, intimacy, and safety. Sure, when it came to my colleagues and clients, I found I could tune in quite well to what the other person was saying, yet with some of my closest relationships...not so much. Since the C.L.E.A.N.S.E. formula is an internal process, you are learning to listen to your body throughout the entire seven steps. Eventually, however, I encourage you to put these skills into practice. Try them out in some of your close and not-so-close relationships.

Please remember to make eye contact and take time for voice-to-voice connection (rather than texting or emailing). It can be so tempting to text your thoughts and feelings. People try to send a feeling through an emoji, like a heart. While it might temporarily touch someone, it doesn't last. That is because we are built for real, true, intimate, raw connection.

I've stopped trying to have a conversation with my husband, mother, or daughters from across the room. During the detox and thereafter, I made a point to sit down and have face-to-face conversations. Part of the reason this worked for us was we made an agreement that we would always ask each other first if we were free or available to have a dialogue. This gave us all a chance to check in with ourselves before communicating. This choice created an environment where everyone felt safe.

Developing your ability to listen involves two skills: the ability to pay attention long enough to repeat what you heard the other person say and being willing to receive energy within the dialogue without taking things as a threat or personally.

MIRRORING

Mirroring is a communication technique in which you repeat back the words of the person you are listening to. If someone says, "I am going to fail this test," you would repeat back, "So you think you are going to fail this test." What often happens in communication is one person tries to fix another. They might say something like "Did you study?" or "No, you will do fine." The challenge is these types of responses can be ways that we, without awareness, control our and other people's emotions. Let's face it: it can be uncomfortable to be around someone who is upset.

> When my oldest daughter was getting ready to drive, I asked her what kind of car she might like to get someday. She replied, "A big SUV."
>
> "Really?" I asked. "Why is that?"
>
> "Because I want to travel and I need lots of seats," she replied.
>
> "Oh, are you taking people with you?" I asked.
>
> "Maybe," she replied.
>
> This conversation went on for a bit, and as you can imagine, it never amounted to anything. However, later I was in a tizzy. My thoughts were running around my brain, creating stories of her leaving, skipping college, getting stranded in some remote place with no cell phone reception. I felt a sudden urge (from my chest) to approach her and let her know (agenda) that her thoughts were unrealistic. When I did react, she replied, "See, Mom, I can't tell you anything." Gulp.

The previous example of disconnection illustrates how important it is for us to tone down reactivity, get into our bodies, and move through the steps before responding to a situation. Not just because failing to do these things breaks down connection but because no one has a chance to feel their whole emotions. Reactions often have a domino effect—when one person snaps, others follow. The only person you control is *you*.

This means you will have to ease up on what you are hearing (content) and instead put more attention and awareness on truly listening without expectations or judgment. Honestly, most of the time the details are irrelevant and bound to change depending on people's moods, their circumstances, and the influences upon them that day.

When I teach my anxiety class, I can easily notice the difference between one student and another—which ones did their body scan before engaging in a conversation and which ones did not. They, too, are amazed at the difference. I often joke with them and say that forgetting your body scan is like having unprotected sex; you take a risk of contracting someone else's energy (e.g., anxiety, anger, or fear) or spewing out some of your own. You know this has occurred if you leave a conversation feeling rattled, distracted, or preoccupied, which is why part of nourishing yourself is doing the scan. It brings you to the present moment, building your immunity to picking up fear.

REDEFINING INDEPENDENCE

You may have learned that independence means you do not need anyone or anything. You can stand on your own two feet with or without him, her, them, or anyone. I am all for empowerment; however, what this mentality creates are roadblocks in your communication. One minute you might act like you are fine, have it all together, and then the next minute feel alone and unsupported. The mindset that you don't need anyone else also puts a little edge on your energy, which may make people reluctant to reach out to or check in with you.

This is because everything you feel and believe registers energetically in your body. To believe you are independent (don't need anyone) can be interpreted by the body as you don't need energy. Relationships are rich with energy, and living your life as if you are better off without them is no different than putting a limit on how much energy you can handle. How this plays out in life is that when energy shows itself (e.g., love, affection, attention), you may be too independent to receive it.

Consider adopting this new definition of independence while moving through the detox: independence is the freedom from the belief that you are separate from the Divine. It is when you can see the good (Divine) in others that your detox will take on new meanings, and rather than live in duality where everything is black or white (good or bad, right or wrong), you will be able to experience the natural flows of connection and disconnection even the healthiest relationships bring. Here are things to look out for, behaviors and viewpoints that keep you separate from the source (Divine):

SEPARATE	CONNECTED
I don't need anyone	I am already connected
I try	I am choosing
I need	I am, we are
Freedom from others	Freedom from self-limiting beliefs
I suffer	I allow

FOSTERING FAITH

Emotional detoxes are all about having faith. Faith is believing in something even if you cannot see it. Many of us neglect or even leave our faiths when we are moving through a hard time. I get it—I was raised Catholic, and much to my mother-in-law's dismay, I asked my husband years ago if we could start attending a new church. That is not to say I wouldn't return to the Catholic Church if it felt right, but we all go through times when we might question our faith. Know that faith is not always about doctrine. The word means having conviction and confidence in what you believe.

The journey with my husband has strengthened my faith. After doing the C.L.E.A.N.S.E. formula in the morning, it wasn't uncommon for me to read Scripture. What I was drawn to was Jesus. I would often wonder how Jesus would respond, and I know in my heart he would say to forgive.

One might say I became a bit of a Holy Roller during my healing journey. With that said, I am a yoga girl, open to all practices that strengthen love. My husband would also tell me about his spiritual experiences. Even though we were not attending church as much as we had hoped to, each of us was committed to having a daily practice of prayer.

I will never forget the day my husband came home from walking the dog and said, "Sheri, I just got this feeling to start praying and praying. I could feel God's presence around me." It would be the day of the horrific shooting in Las Vegas. I often wonder if my husband had a premonition and something inside him knew the world needed prayers.

This is what happens when we start embracing our whole emotions. Rather than contribute to chaos and fear through reactivity, the energy of our emotions gives us awareness. As this grows, we can help heal the planet. Now, with that said, it is important to refrain from praying in fear. This is why I would read Scripture or spiritual texts after moving through the steps of the C.L.E.A.N.S.E. formula. When you pray in fear, you may not receive the healing energy that praying in faith creates.

FORGIVENESS

Although forgiveness falls within the Nourish step, it was something I did early on because I knew that without it I would never be able to embrace my whole emotions. Not forgiving would be a constant distraction.

If it weren't for those darn three kids of ours, I might have stayed under the covers for a month. I remember lying in bed in the middle of the day, crying, my husband by my side wiping the tears away. "I am so sorry," he said. "I will be sorry for the rest of my life." It was at that point I heard myself utter these words: "I forgive you."

Forgiveness is a two-way street. The other person isn't off the hook until he is able to receive it. When we allow ourselves to feel whole emotions, we are in a state of forgiveness because forgiveness is one of the most natural ways to love, not just others but ourselves.

Forgiveness is a choice to move through pain. Nonforgiveness, however, attaches us to pain. I had hoped my husband would someday be able to receive forgiveness, because when you receive the energy of forgiveness from others, you are letting them know that what they are offering is valuable and sacred. If you are riddled with guilt, shame, and fear (toxicity), receiving forgiveness will be difficult to do. As you connect to your whole emotions, forgiveness will follow—the only way to put it to a halt is to resort to reactivity. Forgiveness is a process; however, to set it in motion, all you need to do is make the choice to heal, and that means embracing your whole emotions.

Honestly, receiving is way more challenging. Think about it. If you ever caused someone else's pain and he or she forgave you, I bet it was hard to receive. Most people don't receive forgiveness, and that is a shame, because it creates such a strain on a relationship. Once you receive forgiveness, you will see living in a state of nonforgiveness is the most unnatural way to be.

I know some people couldn't quite grasp how I could forgive my husband so early on. What they might not have known is that it would be the energy of forgiveness that would give me the courage and strength to move through the insurmountable pain and sadness. Otherwise, I risked spending a lifetime living in the past. Sure, I would have gotten older and life would have moved on. However, nothing changes until the energy of your emotions digest. What other people might not have understood was that leaving forgiveness on the table meant having to revisit the past. The focus would then be on "Should I forgive him? Am I ready?" rather than "How am I feeling right now? What am I noticing, and in what way can I allow myself to be present to today?" Forgiveness took the focus off him and put it on me.

RECAP

- Offer a daily appreciation aloud to someone.
- Develop your gaze.
- Let go of agendas; be genuine.
- Practice listening without judgment.
- Pray in faith, not fear.
- Set the intention to heal, and forgiveness will follow.

CLEANSING TIP: RECEIVING ENERGY

This cleansing tip will teach you how to receive energy. Place the palms of your hands together and rub them vigorously, like you are rolling Play-Doh between your hands. Do this while sitting up tall for about twenty seconds, creating a lot of friction. Then separate your hands and hover one over your heart and the other over your throat. Close your eyes and breathe. If you don't feel anything, redo the process, starting by rubbing your hands vigorously again. Breathe, notice, and feel the vibration pulsating into your heart and throat. Notice how being able to receive energy means you must be relaxed and open—this is what the state of forgiveness feels like.

C.L.E.A.N.S.E. STEP 6: SURRENDER

"The first step toward change is awareness.
The second step is acceptance."

—Nathaniel Branden

Now that you have raised your energetic vibration by digesting your emotions, activated joy, and learned some new skills from the Nourish step, you are ready to put an end to old patterns. These ways of thinking and behaving don't suit you anymore. This is because you have outgrown them. You have matured in how you handle your emotions, and therefore hanging onto old ways of reacting is pointless. Moving back to your organic self is about learning to live your life without all the additives. Only instead of chemicals and pesticides, you are learning to live without the narratives of remarks, comments, and criticisms that may have been circulating in your head. This will all help you to live with more ease, which is discussed in Step 7.

For now, my hope is you are realizing how valuable your emotions are and that therefore you don't have to settle for less. You can have the life you desire. This step is about closure. Yes, you will be saying adios to the artificial sweeteners reactivity can bring. The purpose of surrender is not to get rid of your emotions but to allow healing and wellness to come into being. In this step, you will learn about why I don't believe in letting go, the role of Mother Earth in your detox, how to ditch the guilt (finally), and how to rinse the residue of unprocessed pain. So, take the final bow and let's close the curtain on all the drama—it is time to surrender.

LET IT FLOW

For years I told myself to let it go. I would cringe at something minor like the sound of the potato chip bag crinkling next to me while I was trying to watch TV and think, *Sheri, let it go.* Meanwhile, I would feel tension in my jaw as I sat exhausted on the couch after a long day. I also worked hard at letting go of people-pleasing. Maybe if I smiled more, offered compliments, or volunteered to wash all the dishes at the house party, they would like me more… *Sheri, let it go.*

Letting go doesn't work. Haven't you noticed? This is because the process forces you to pay attention to the thing you want to get rid of (e.g., being uptight, people not liking you).

When it comes to surrender, it is not about letting it go but rather letting it flow—the "it" being our whole emotions. With that said, there is nothing wrong with asking someone to turn the TV up so you can hear over the potato chip crunching! However, we all know it's not about the potato chips—it's about controlling our emotions through reactivity.

THE SECRET IS OUT

During your emotional detox, one of the ways you'll surrender is to Mother Earth, because she is one of the most universally trusted healers. We can all agree that the earth holds extraordinary healing abilities. Step into the ocean, hold a crystal in your hand, or watch the dry earth soak up a steady rain, and you'll know what I mean. Keep in mind, this also activates joy as a powerful cleanser, and so when you surrender to Mother Earth, you are contributing this incredible joy to her healing capacities.

When you were growing up, did you ever keep a secret from your mother? Perhaps you held back some of the details or modified a story so that you would not upset her. It might take years, but I find many of these secrets leak out—directly or indirectly. Moms are known for their ability to pick up on subtle body language or notice when something isn't quite in its place.

Mother Earth works in the same way. We may not tell her about our pain or admit our fears and anxieties, but that doesn't mean she doesn't sense and feel them. Studies like those described in Peter Tompkins and Christopher Bird's *The Secret Life of Plants* show that plants grow significantly better when exposed to pleasing sounds like classical music.

Mother Earth does the same thing as the plants in these studies. She leans into our vibration, and the quality of these vibrations matters. When we repeat words that are negative or low in energy, they contaminate our environment just as smoke or chemicals do. When we surrender to Mother Earth, we are sending a message of love and respect. We love and respect her so much we are willing to have an honest, open, and healing relationship with her. This means instead of holding back your emotions, bless Mother Earth by offering her your pure, whole emotions.

EVOLVING YOUR INHALE

Our inhale is rich with nutrients. We know this because when we inhale, something inside us shifts. Things such as your courage, presence, and compassion tend to grow. You may have experienced this— the immense joy of giving birth or earning a degree after years of study.

As you spend time with the C.L.E.A.N.S.E. steps, you will evolve in other ways—training mind and body to become more present. As this occurs, your ability to accept and trust things as they are will increase.

In the Emit step, you learned how to stay centered through your exhale and then moved to Activate Joy (Step 4) by inhaling and expanding your heart and higher mind (third eye). Then in Step 5, you nourished on exhale by offering an appreciation. Now you are ready to take this all one step (or breath) further. Just as you can pick up a metal object with a magnet, your inhale gives you the means to draw away layers of fear, anxiety, and grief you have been holding onto. Remember, as you strip the reactivity, underneath it all are your beautiful, whole emotions. Be generous with your release. Include letting the belief that you are a victim flow. Overfocusing on your exhale without awareness can perpetuate this type of thinking. You'll know this because you might feel a bit wounded.

When I noticed a wounded feeling (heartbreak, insecurity), I would choose to focus on my inhale and make way for new states of being. I knew if I allowed myself to think and feel as if I were a victim, this could potentially sabotage my progress. It would be through my inhale that I would be able to bust the seams of these bodily (energetic) expectations.

Try this:

- Take a moment now and close your eyes.

- Allow your shoulders to relax, and deepen your breath by inhaling and exhaling through your nose. Connect to your core on the exhale, and observe your body on inhale.

- Do this without force. The more you observe your inhale, the more expansive it becomes.

MOVING BEYOND YOUR COMFORT ZONE

Moving beyond your comfort zone means you have to surrender some attitudes. One I have seen in my clients is a "that ship has sailed" mindset. This attitude forces them to concentrate on some areas while neglecting others. I get it; I did it too. I became well versed in my professional studies, yet when it came to my marriage, I managed to turn a blind eye. This is because at the time it seemed useless to bring up what was bothering me or how I was feeling.

What the emotional detox taught me is that it is never too late—darling, that ship has not sailed. As you develop your inhale, I want you to imagine yourself zooming in on what it is you would like to create in your life. When you overfocus on your exhale, your inhale gets cut short. This means you have overfocused on what has happened *to you* rather than what is happening *for you*.

Picture yourself right now smelling a beautiful flower. Notice what happens to your inhale. Notice how your inhale naturally expands as you take in the flower's natural scent. When you feel old thoughts and beliefs tugging at you, I encourage you to breathe like you are smelling something wonderful. This is what it is going to feel like to shred those old patterns—smooth, like butter.

> One of the things I chose to surrender during the detox was the way I used to overexplain myself. My children were growing older and letting me know my lectures were overkill. It was through the development and connection to my inhale that I began to let this behavior go. As a result, my teens rose to the occasion—they received my shift as an opportunity to show me that they didn't need my lectures anymore.

Expanding our inhale is how we surrender old patterns. The ability to observe increases the ability to pay attention to the moment. When we are observing our inhale, we can't hold onto lower vibrational thoughts (e.g., "I can't") and circumstances. We have no choice but to let them go—if we go back to the negative, we'll distract ourselves from the inhale and return to reactivity. Let's apply this to surrendering guilt.

THE GUILTY HABIT

We know we are experiencing guilt when we "feel bad." It is important that we allow ourselves to surrender guilt because guilt will create resistance toward being vulnerable, and without vulnerability it will be difficult to get in touch with raw emotions. Guilt is like putting a lid on reactivity—it pushes it down. As guilt is submerged, reactivity is likely to increase or express itself through intense emotions, such as anger, finger-pointing, or sarcasm.

Guilt is one emotion that can push us to places we don't want to be—I have watched people give others the benefit of the doubt too many times because of guilt. Rather than trust their instincts they allow guilt to decide how long they will suffer. Perhaps a relationship needs to end or a transition needs to be made. If you find yourself controlling or managing a situation through guilt ("I should" or "I shouldn't"), then somewhere along the way you veered off. You lost your ability to trust yourself and instead took the path of self-abuse. We've all been there—don't you think I knew something was off in my marriage? I did, and one of the ways I avoided dealing with it was to be a slave to guilt. I felt bad for spending money, taking time for myself, having sex, not having sex, making a lousy dinner, going to bed too early, working too late, missing one of my kids' field trips, or not calling my mother. Guilt makes us feel like we can never do or be enough.

Guilt in itself is not bad; it is our reaction to heavy, suppressed emotions that keeps us tethered to toxicity. Guilt is often tied into a fear of disappointing others. We hold off on the experience of our emotions for the sake of others. Here is the thing: there is nothing we can *do* about it, but we can choose to *be*, and the C.L.E.A.N.S.E. formula offers a way of being.

SELF-ACCEPTANCE

According to Leon F. Seltzer, PhD, in *Psychology Today*, self-esteem and self-acceptance are not the same. He writes, "Whereas self-esteem refers specifically to how valuable, or worthwhile, we see ourselves... self-acceptance is unconditional, free of any qualification. We can recognize our weaknesses, limitations, and foibles, but this awareness in no way interferes with our ability to fully accept ourselves."

Here is what the detox taught me. As you cleanse toxicity from your body, you no longer need to accept your perceived faults because that was all a reaction in the first place. In other words, seeing faults is a reaction. To find defects, you must run a narrative in your head that includes the belief that something or someone is better than you—that you have failed, you are not good enough, or you could have done better. The moment you stop trying so hard (reaction) to hold it all together and you surrender all the joy you have tapped into to Mother Earth, you will begin to move into states of healing.

Over the years, I have worked with many fatherless or motherless clients. Perhaps they grew up in a single-parent home or one parent was far more present than the other. As I move them through the C.L.E.A.N.S.E. formula, the belief that they were not enough often surfaces—that somehow the choices their parents made were somehow their fault. It would be through learning the difference between self-esteem and self-acceptance that they would begin to surrender these old ways of viewing things.

Coming back to your organic self means you will be surrendering any tendencies to compare yourself to others. This means no more measuring up. This will be difficult for those who have had strong academic training. Typically school is the place where you learn to compare yourself to others to cope with the variety of pressures. The bottom line is that whether it is fitting into a family, friendship circle, trade, or community, practicing self-acceptance can help you loosen the expectation that you should be a certain way to be accepted for who you are.

One of the most common unconscious fears is the fear of making a mistake. As a result, we learn to confuse our mistakes for our identity. Rather than experience (digest) the emotions that are influenced by our decisions, we instead react to them, and one of the ways this happens is that we hand out our own punishment. This often comes through harsh criticisms. Without awareness, these judgments knock down your self-esteem, making self-acceptance seem like a tall order.

Getting clear on the difference between the two will help you surrender old tendencies while placing your focus on what you would like to inhale in your life (self-acceptance). Through self-acceptance, self-esteem will naturally follow. In many ways, we have been working way too hard to feel worthy. We have overdone the self-improvement fad. Your worth is one of the most natural parts of who you are, and because you exist you are worthy. The following breakdown will help you understand the difference between the two concepts.

SELF-ESTEEM	SELF-ACCEPTANCE
Strength focused	Compassion focused
Concentrates on self-image	Concentrates on self-awareness
Builds confidence	Builds relationships
Increases ability to try new things	Increases ability to tolerate differences
Feeds off measurements	Feeds on resilience
Intertwines with needing	Intertwines with trusting

LOVE WINS

To make the most of your emotional detox experience, I suggest you surrender the notion that you need a reason to detox. Much of this mindset has been pushed through our culture through the marketing of "self-improvement." You don't have to improve yourself; you must *be* yourself. That means digesting your emotions in the absence of reactivity. This is the purest form of you.

Doubting whether you "need" to digest your emotions is no different than asking, "Do I need a bridge between my mind and my body?" The link between your brain and body is you. Since science has taught us about inherited trauma, there may not be a specific event that leads you to detox. It may have nothing to do with your current set of circumstances. By moving through the steps, I have realized a good majority of our reactivity is due to triggered trauma. To support the process, I suggest you think of your emotional detox as a service rather than a treatment.

In the beginning, moving through the steps seemed like a form of treatment. Once I got to the Surrender step, this all would change. Rather than seeing clearing reactivity as a step, I saw it as a service to myself and my family. It was a way for me to contribute to (rather than prevent) what was happening. It turned out that I didn't need to work so hard to try to make everything go smoothly. Living in wholeness was my service. As a result, many blessings followed.

Pastor Rick Warren wrote, "Jesus…measured greatness in terms of service, not status. God determines your greatness by how many people you serve, not how many people serve you." It would be through the shedding of my tears that I would reveal one of my greatest fears: to be upfront about my feelings. I felt like I would be screwing up if I were to be honest about the way I was feeling (e.g., frustrated, tired, grumpy). Ironically it would be my husband who would help me heal this fear, looking me straight in the eyes and saying, "You don't ever have to worry about making a mistake with me. I love you the way you are; you don't ever have to change." Although it was strange that the one person who betrayed me was simultaneously loving me, it was in that moment that I realized how powerful love is, and from that point on, my mantra became "Love wins."

CLOSURE

Closure means something has been completed. There is an end point to what has happened. You may choose to end a job or finally make a decision to buy a new car. When it comes to relationships, having closure looks different. It means an old way of seeing things has ended. Perhaps you saw your partner one way and after the honeymoon was over your perspective changed. For this reason, closure takes time. This is because there are some things for you to know and learn. To reach true closure, you will find you need to go through the process of cultivating self-awareness and self-acceptance.

For me, gaining closure was twofold. I had to take responsibility for my part in the breakdown of our marriage, and I needed to do it with self-compassion rather than self-destruction. Whenever I did mess up—like saying something hurtful in the heat of an argument—I was hard on myself, so my emotions were never given the chance to become fully digested. As a result, the energy stayed the same. Having closure meant taking responsibility for what I was feeling by paying more attention to my bodily feedback.

If you find your levels of reactivity keep spiking, then you may be missing your bodily messages. (This will be discussed more in the Ease step.) In my case, I had to take responsibility for my fatigue, not just physical but the mental exhaustion it sometimes takes to raise a family. This meant I needed to learn how to say no, to let go of trying to get everything done and then some, and to celebrate healthy ways of living (e.g., exercise, healthy eating) rather than seeing them as a chore.

As you move through these steps, you are raising your levels of self-awareness. It is your intentions, self-awareness, discipline, and self-acceptance that propel this C.L.E.A.N.S.E. formula. As your body surrenders old ways of being and seeing things, you are changing (energetically) inside and out. Therefore, similar to how adolescents feel extra tired when their brains are growing and changing and need extra rest, you too might need some extra TLC.

Surrendering old parts while integrating new asks you to be kind and loving to yourself. Give yourself permission to take a break, pause, and breathe. There were many times I had to be okay with making sandwiches and soup for dinner, plopping on the couch, and easing up on timelines. Otherwise, I risked pushing myself to the limit, snapping at the people who were trying to support me and feeling disappointed in the way I handled it.

Closure did not come from completing the past but from my willingness to receive and carry on the wisdom. By expanding my inhale, I found it easier to make closure less about ending a chapter and more about starting a new one. If I felt stuck or glued to the ending rather than open and excited about a new beginning, I would ask, *What are you afraid of?* Then whatever followed would be acknowledged by my exhale and digested through my inhale.

TOO MUCH DRESSING

Over the course of the year following the affair, I thought and talked less about what happened. Although I would continue to honor the process, I made a conscious decision to be mindful of what and when I shared with others. I even paid attention to the moments when I wanted to share but held myself back. It was in those moments that I realized I had a choice, either to lead a conversation from my past or be connected to the moment. Like a salad with too much dressing, oversharing is not a good thing—if you overshare your story, telling everyone you encounter, it will interfere with the surrendering process.

When I was riding in the car listening to the audiobook *Why People Don't Heal and How They Can* by medical intuitive Caroline Myss, I heard, "Investing our energy into the past is like trying to keep a dead corpse alive. The past doesn't provide your life force only the present does." Now I ask, "What are you investing in—the past or the now?" I chose the now repeatedly until it had become habituated—there was no point in asking because body and spirit were clear on my preference.

RECAP

- Rather than let go, let flow.
- Surrender to Mother Earth for healing and to contribute your joy.
- Evolve your inhale by expanding your lungs; imagine smelling a beautiful flower.
- Replace guilt with acceptance.
- Know you are changing inside and out; give yourself time, space, and extra TLC as fatigue may set in.
- Allow closure, take responsibility for your part, accept the wisdom, and pass it on.

CLEANSING TIP: PRAY

As you evolve your inhale, you will be able to reach higher states of being and meditation. This is also an ideal time to pray. To pray means to devote some time to giving praise to your higher creator. It is a devotional practice. The Lord's Prayer or a goddess or Mother Earth prayer might feel right for you. I suggest you find one, memorize it, and recite it daily. Otherwise, you might feel alone in this process and, darling, you are way more supported than you might realize. Your prayer may sound something like this: *I call upon you, Jesus, the healer, son of God, to be in my life today, as well as in the lives of _____.*
I humbly bow to your divine light and ask for your holy presence to be in me and around me (and my family, community) today and every day and allow me and Mother Earth to be fully cleansed by the healing powers of your unconditional love, which I am choosing to receive fully now. Amen.

C.L.E.A.N.S.E. STEP 7: EASE

*"Come to me, all you who are weary and burdened,
and I will give you rest. Take my yoke upon you
and learn from me, for I am gentle and humble in
heart, and you will find rest for your souls."*

—Matthew 11:28–29

In this final step, you will ask yourself, *If I am not reacting, what am I doing instead?* The answer is focusing on how you feel. It is your raw feelings (rather than your thoughts) that bring more peace and ease into your life. This step is loaded with simple tips for day-to-day living, as well as insight on how to handle some of the more complicated things that bring unease and disharmony. You will learn how to handle criticism, as well as how to ask for your needs without fear and struggle. This step will also address that five-letter word so many of us avoid: *trust*. You will learn what trust is about and how to show up for love even after you have been betrayed.

Before giving you some tips on how to live a life with more ease, it is important that we begin by learning how to develop trust. Without trust you are likely to turn to some of the following tools and strategies to cope with fear. Trust is the foundation for your tools, not the outcome.

BUILDING TRUST

Trust happens when you communicate with your feelings rather than your fears. It is a firm belief in the reliability of something or someone. You can trust that what someone says or does is true. Whether you are looking to gain back someone's trust or wondering how to trust after being betrayed, remember that it doesn't begin with the other person, it begins with you. Building trust takes three key ingredients: vulnerability (feeling), boundaries, and compassion.

Every year my husband and I go on two separate weekend excursions. My husband goes hiking with the guys, while the girls and I spend a weekend on a working farm. During the last visit, I woke up to an emergency text. "Mom, mom, mom," it read, "emergency, go to the pool now." Although everything turned out fine, for about ten minutes I couldn't find my older daughters, and with only a text announcing an emergency, there were a million fearful thoughts running through my head. For the rest of the weekend, I was on edge. However, when my husband texted me, I responded with "Everything is fine, love ya." Everything did seem fine until I pulled into the driveway, unpacked the car, went into the house, and heard how awesome his weekend had been. I was upset—he had no clue what I had gone through! That's when he responded, "How do you expect me to read between the lines, Sheri? You told me you were fine."

What I learned about developing trust that weekend is it will never happen when we are not being honest with our feelings. By telling my husband that everything was fine when my body was in high reactivity, I was falling into old patterns of protecting rather than feeling my feelings. If I could do it again, I would have said, "When I received that text, I felt terrified, scared, and alone." When we communicate with our pure emotions rather than protect through reactivity, trust begins to take root. Sure, communicating my true feelings might have spiked some sensations in my body. So if you're in a similar situation, return to the beginning of the formula, follow all seven steps, and I promise ease will follow.

BOUNDARIES

Think of boundaries as an internal platform. When they are in place, this increases your ability to see yourself and your surroundings. Without them you are more likely to skip or disregard what you are sensing and feeling. If you have ever had people talk your ear off, to the point where they disregard your body language and signals of discomfort, you know what I mean.

They have approached you without tuning into their internal boundaries. Therefore, they cannot properly read the conversation. They might think that you are fine with listening. Maybe they haven't been taught the proper social skills. However, I believe a huge part of social awareness is knowing how to pay attention and note your bodily sensations (emotions). It is hard to do that without boundaries; we risk misinterpreting the energy we feel.

We cannot develop trust by overfocusing on another person—it does not work that way. Judgment is a reaction, and like all reactions it creates stagnation of emotions. When this occurs, we may not see the whole picture. No relationship can flourish if we are in a state of reactivity.

I had trust issues with my husband long before the affair. I know this now because I felt he wasn't there for me. Learning how to set boundaries by surrendering the behavior of overfocusing on him and instead developing my trust allowed me to get to know the real him and all that he was capable of.

Those of us who grew up in environments that were inconsistent and unstable know what I mean. It's not that I didn't have food on my plate and loving parents, but energetically, to take care of myself, I learned to overfocus on what was happening outside of me. This often occurs when there is addiction in the home—you don't know what to expect, so you become an expert at overfocusing on others.

Setting boundaries is an internal experience. It pulls us back to the center. Rather than spend time trying to figure out, accuse, or analyze another person, we focus on our energy. This is because reactions (like accusing) make us mistrust energy. We will never develop trust this way. It is not our job to decide if someone else is worthy; it is our job to practice learning how to trust our emotions. One way to do that is through the C.L.E.A.N.S.E. formula.

During our healing journey, my husband and I were also facing some financial challenges. We dipped into our savings account to pay the bills. We both knew that solution could only last so long. We also knew that without trust it didn't matter how much money we had—things would still feel the same—so we focused on building trust instead. Over a year into the process my husband shared that he had many days when he worried about money yet felt such a strong connection to God. As he put it, "I feel like He is in my back pocket and everything is going to be fine." Fourteen months after finding out about the affair, both my husband and I were offered substantial job opportunities. Things worked out far better than expected.

One way to set internal boundaries is to notice when you are over-focusing on others or your problems. Rather than go into judgment, try this:

- Find your center by lengthening your back and connecting to your core (navel, pelvic floor).

- Lift your pelvic floor (engaging the muscles you use to go to the bathroom) as you exhale.

- Be sure to release your jaw.

- Focus on how you feel. If you sense reactivity (e.g., upper-chest breathing), return to the beginning of the formula and move through the steps a second time.

This will bring you back to the present moment where trust grows.

Without a core connection, we don't know what we are stepping into. I find people with loose boundaries are more apt to go to people-pleasing or trying to fix or control others. They might be quick to say "Chill out," dominate, interrupt, or rearrange their schedule. In their minds, they are helping. What ends up happening is they never learn how to trust the flow of their emotions. Their actions and reactions stop or prevent. This is no different than saying to your body, "I don't trust what I am feeling, so quick, make it stop or else..." Loose boundaries disrupt energy rather than complete it.

As you practice setting boundaries, your mind, body, and spirit begin to merge. This gives you a heightened sense of knowing and trusting—maybe the courage to speak up, make a decision, or change. Trust comforts us while giving a sense that life may hold some divine guidance or blessings.

TENDING TO VULNERABILITY

Once you draw boundaries within yourself, the next step is to allow yourself to be vulnerable. This means your willingness to expose your heart. Exposing your heart is no different than saying, *I can show up as I am, and everything will still be okay.* Vulnerability is a state of feeling bare, open, and exposed. If you are running a fearful narrative in your head (*I am so weak, I don't know how much I can take*), that is not vulnerability—it is a reaction to fear.

Now with that said, I want you to know vulnerability often comes with a little uncertainty and nervousness. This is because you are on the cusp of transformation. It is important that you notice if you react to your nervousness or uncertainty rather than allow it to surface. Trust develops as you practice noticing the difference between reactivity and vulnerability; with growth comes discomfort.

When I teach yoga, I often have students lie flat on the floor with a bolster or block underneath their mid-backs and a pillow underneath their heads. Their buttocks stay on the floor. This position opens up the heart, chest, and throat. It allows them to feel what it is like to experience vulnerability without reactivity. Vulnerability is something to experience rather than do. It is the art of watching ourselves develop courage and trust.

This is important because when you apply the tools and strategies listed in this step, they will be far more effective as you are developing your ability to be more vulnerable. Let me give an example.

Imagine if a child was feeling sad and upset. You could either go up to that child and ask what is the matter or you could rub her back and tell her everything is going to be okay. One is not better than the other. However, when you ask what is the matter, you are asking yourself and, in this example, the child to revisit the past. Vulnerability, love, and ease live in the moment. By giving yourself an opportunity

PART II: THE C.L.E.A.N.S.E. FORMULA

to be present to what is happening without needing to fix or figure it out, you are offering yourself (or another) love and compassion during a vulnerable state. When you are in a state of vulnerability, you are touching base with your core self and your raw emotions. There is a big difference between telling someone everything is going to be okay when he or she is in a state of vulnerability as opposed to reactivity. This is the same for you.

When you apply the following eight renewal tools to a state of vulnerability, you are speaking to the pure you—the part of you that is unfiltered and open to receiving love, growth, and healing.

EIGHT WAYS TO RENEW ENERGY

Here are some tools and strategies for taking care of yourself in a loving and compassionate way. Emotional detoxes are all about increasing compassion for yourself and others. Know the tools and strategies that follow are a guideline. You don't have to do them all! You will find that once you develop trust, you will become more open and willing to practice these tools.

ONE: SHOWING UP WITH PRESENCE

One of the most important tools for living with more ease is to pay attention to how you show up to the moment. This means increasing your ability to observe your breath, witnessing your bodily sensations, and owning your levels of reactivity by taking yourself through the steps. Ask: *What is my intention for showing up?* Intend to show up willing to listen, present, and respectful of the energy of the emotions that are being revealed. Just as you might hold the door open for the person behind you as a sign of respect, the way in which you pause and breathe is a way to honor the presence of your sensations (emotions).

TWO: ONE THING AT A TIME

Creating ease means to pause, tune in to the moment, and let yourself do one thing at a time. Put away your cell phone, refrain from texting or checking your emails, and focus on what is happening right now. If you must, let people know you are working and won't be responding to any texts for a certain period. You cannot create ease and take care of everything else at the same time. The cool part is you will get more done because you are gaining energy from your emotions by being present.

THREE: KNOW WHERE YOUR PAUSE BUTTON IS

Bringing more ease means knowing where your pause button is. Contrary to what many of us have been taught, to stop and think about what is happening does little when it comes to digesting your emotions. Your pause button is not in your brain, it is in your navel. The area around your navel is also referred to as your power center or solar plexus area. It is the area where you can experience the feeling that you have been kicked in the gut or the wind has been knocked out of your sails. When you feel like your mind is running away from you or you feel overwhelmed or anxious, press your navel toward your spine as you might press the brake pedal in your car. This will help create more space between your thoughts and get you to regulate your breathing.

FOUR: USE MORE VISUALIZATIONS

One of the best ways to bring more ease into your life is to visualize. This doesn't mean you need to be an artist. The creative part of you is your ability to use your imagination. Albert Einstein said, "The true sign of intelligence is not knowledge but imagination." This is what makes guided meditations so powerful. To support your emotional flow, visualize images of nature. Imagine water running smoothly in a stream, glistening, cleansing, and purifying itself as it brushes along the dirt and rocks. See a beautiful tree, moving its branches, growing strong and tall as it weathers through storms of rage, anger, and deep sadness. See how dedicated and strong the earth is.

> In my daily C.L.E.A.N.S.E. practice, I always end with a visualization of seeing myself in a beautiful place or doing what I love. I might picture myself running on the beach with one of my children.

FIVE: DO THINGS YOU ENJOY

Hobbies can be a great source of enjoyment—anything from bike riding to gardening, making floral arrangements, knitting, writing, reading, dancing, or practicing yoga. During my emotional detox, I started taking dance classes. To increase ease, notice when life becomes robotic (routine) or serious. Make time to let your hair down, spend time with friends, and allow yourself to enjoy the simple pleasures in life.

SIX: DECLUTTER AND GET ORGANIZED

Do you have a closet or corner of a room that every time you pass, your emotions feel bound up? Bound-up emotions feel like a brick wall—you just stop breathing and distract yourself from the process. Pay attention to how clutter affects the movement of your emotions. Ask yourself, "What am I storing?" Be curious about how much resistance you must maintain to be able to carry on with a business-as-usual approach. Here is the good news. Don't be surprised while practicing the formula if you take on some of these mini projects (i.e., clearing out clutter). I know for me I got on quite a roll cleaning out the toy bin and kitchen cabinets. *What freedom!*

SEVEN: MINDFUL EATING

To be mindful means to pay attention on purpose without judgment. As you learn to digest your emotions more fluidly, your relationship with food will also change. You will learn it is better to eat mindfully, with full attention rather than shoving your food quietly down your throat. I suggest selecting one meal a day where you will eat without any distractions (TV, phone, etc.). Sit in a chair for God's sake, feel your feet touch the ground. Chew your food slowly and savor its flavor.

EIGHT: DEVELOP RITUALS

Rituals are different from routines. Routines are tasks we do daily like brushing our teeth and eating meals. Rituals are things that enhance our ability to connect—with others or the Divine. Things like saying a prayer before dinner, writing down what you are grateful for, lighting a candle, making soup on Sundays, or leaving a love note.

When done with intention to connect, rituals invite peace into your heart and home. In many ways, the C.L.E.A.N.S.E. formula has become a ritual for me, as I hope it will for you. Like joy, rituals foster resiliency. If you are concerned about negativity around you or those you love, rituals are a nice way to overcome these heavy energies. I recommend creating a ritual for letting go of the day.

LETTING-GO RITUALS

Here are some of my favorite letting-go rituals. Pick the ones that feel best for you.

- Listen to calming music during your commute, while you make dinner, or before you fall asleep.
- Go for a walk and call it your "letting-go" walk.
- Visualize. Release the day by imagining a strong wind whisking away all your fears and worries. See yourself smiling and breathing in a place that offers you ease—in a meadow, by a pond, or near the ocean.
- Recite a mantra. One of my favorite mantras at the end of the day is "and so be it," which is the translation for *amen*. In my book *Mantras Made Easy*, there are over one hundred and fifty mantras for you to explore. I recommend that you select one and recite it daily, a minimum of ten times in a row for forty days. This can be a morning and evening ritual.
- Meditate. Sit in a comfortable, seated position in a low-lit room with your eyes closed. It is best if you sit so you don't fall asleep. Observe your body and breath without judgment. If you like, you can follow a guided meditation or listen to soft, soothing music. Sounds of nature can help you relax.

EXPRESSING YOUR NEEDS

As you develop trust, you will find it easier to ask to have your needs met. This is an important part of living with more ease, because in the past you might have felt wrong or undeserving. The C.L.E.A.N.S.E. formula will help you develop the courage. To begin, understand the difference between what you need to survive and what you need to thrive.

WHAT YOU NEED TO SURVIVE	WHAT YOU NEED TO THRIVE
Food	Connection (hugs, kisses)
Water	Emotional flow (feeling whole emotions)
Shelter	Feeling grounded and safe (boundaries)

Add the ones that are meaningful for you.

CHOOSING YOUR FLAVOR

Just as it's easier to digest a small vanilla ice cream cone than a sundae loaded with hot fudge, peanut butter cups, and whipped cream, some of the language we choose to speak may require more energy to emotionally digest. Here are some statements that interfere with ease contrasted with language that will support it:

DEPLETING LANGUAGE	UPLIFTING LANGUAGE
I can't, I try, I should…	I choose…
You always…	I am feeling…
Fine. *Whatever.*	That works for me.
It's okay.	Yes.
Never, should, could, always…	I will, I am, I have…

IT'S NOTHING PERSONAL

As you begin to apply the detox mindset to your life, you will see others differently. Rather than think "He is so angry" or "She is so uptight," you will see people as being in a state of reactivity—and now you know that can be a painful place to be! You will also notice the presence or absence of reactivity in your responses. Rather than resort to old ways of defensiveness, criticism, withdrawal, or judgment, we can use the C.L.E.A.N.S.E. formula to remind us that our primary goal is to reduce reactivity. From there we can learn how to give and receive feedback without disconnecting from others. Here is a chart that shows how you can transform criticism into expressing your feelings:

CRITICISM	FEEDBACK
You were ten minutes late.	When you arrive on time, it makes me feel like you care.
You never notice what I do well.	Thank you for appreciating my dinner.
I do everything around here.	How I am feeling right now is overwhelmed and frustrated.

RECAP

- Notice if you are overfocusing on others or your problems.

- Redirect awareness to self.

- Talk about how you *feel* (e.g., scared, unsafe) not what you *think*.

- Create internal boundaries by connecting to your core.

- Develop trust by getting to know your energy through self-care.

- Incorporate tools and strategies for increasing ease.

- Transform criticism into expressing your needs.

CLEANSING TIP: BLESS YOUR WATER

Before drinking a glass of water, place your hand over the top and whisper or imagine beautiful words and images. Something as simple as "thank you" or saying the words "I love you" are ways you can send your body beautiful messages. Here is the research on how this works:

As described in his book *The Hidden Messages in Water,* Masaru Emoto decided to freeze water and look at it with a high-powered microscope. He experimented with the water, placing different words on the containers, playing different sounds and lyrics of music, and showing the water pictures. What he found was that water has consciousness. When the water was offered kind words and images, the ice appeared crystal-like, forming magical shapes. On the other hand, when the water was offered hateful words or violent lyrics, it became fragmented, torn, and discolored with a sick appearance. This research suggests that the words you say make an impact, and because the human body is 60 percent water, the words you choose affect your inner aquarium.

PART III
MANIFESTING JOY

THE C.L.E.A.N.S.E. FORMULA DOES MORE THAN REDUCE TOXICITY. IT IS ALSO A PRACTICE OF MANIFESTING! NOW, IF YOU ARE LIKE ME, I LOVED *THE SECRET*. THE BOOK AND MOVIE ARE BASED ON THE LAW OF ATTRACTION AND GOT PEOPLE TO PAY ATTENTION TO THE POWER OF THEIR PRE-DOMINANT THOUGHTS. THE LAW TEACHES THAT WHAT WE FOCUS ON WE ATTRACT, BUT ACCORDING TO DEEPAK CHOPRA, THE LAW OF REFLECTION IS EVEN MORE USEFUL: "THIS LAW STATES THAT THE WHOLE SITUATION AROUND YOU IS YOU. 'I AM WHAT I SEE. WHAT I SEE IS ME.'"

Gulp.

I reflected on this quite a bit and remember a moment during my emotional crisis when I heard a voice in my head ask, *Did I create this?* Before you shout "Boo!" and throw spitballs at me, I admit (accept) while my husband was out having an affair, I was busy protecting myself through fearful thinking. I had no idea (consciously) about the affair, but what I did know was that something was not right. Had I digested (rather than reacted to) my whole emotions, I might have had the space to express how I was feeling. For example, I might have said, "I feel disconnected from you and this makes me feel alone." At the time, I was too afraid; I thought that if I said the wrong thing, he would leave. Little did I know my worst fears had already happened.

The C.L.E.A.N.S.E. formula teaches you how to feel again. It breaks down those inner walls of fear (remember Step 3 shows you how to do this with sound). It will be difficult to focus in a new way without the energy of your whole emotions. Without this energy, you are likely to default to old patterns of fear. When you choose to move through the steps, eventually focusing on activating joy, you are aligning with both the law of attraction and the law of reflection.

> I would find out later that my husband was also fearful of losing me. He would tell me he didn't feel good enough. After all that was said and done, I don't think he ever expected me to choose him, and perhaps I didn't expect I would either. Love has a funny way of surprising us, and I am grateful it does.

We now know that our emotions are what we are born with; reactivity is what we learn. To help you stick with the program, it is important for you to know some ways people have sabotaged their progress. Think of it like a diet. You do great for a while and slowly fall off the wagon. Knowing this is also the formula for manifesting will help keep you on track. Yet before heading in that direction, it is important for you to be aware of how emotional detoxes get sabotaged.

CHAPTER 6
HOW EMOTIONAL DETOXES GET SABOTAGED

"The essence of spiritual life is simply to use our free will properly."

—Radhanath Swami

Most self-sabotaging behaviors are learned. I think of them like artificial sweeteners—they offer you few nutrients and get you hooked on quick fixes for gaining energy. The challenge is these behaviors can be addictive and they interfere with your manifesting potential. Because they are a way to control your emotions (which is toxic) rather than feel them, a false sense of security often goes with self-sabotaging behaviors. However, as you further practice how to process your emotions, these habits and tendencies will dissipate.

In this chapter, you'll learn some things to look out for—ways in which you might unconsciously sabotage your progress. Some of these things include how you might be isolating yourself, misusing your free will, attaching to pain, engineering the moment, relying on imaginary hits, absorbing other people's energy, staying loyal to low energy, and taxing yourself. Know that the moment you become aware, you have already shifted directions.

DISCONNECTION

Disconnection happens when you separate yourself from feeling. You can do this by excluding yourself from people and/or nature. You can also find ways to prevent yourself from feeling by doing things such as working extra hours, abusing alcohol, staying up late so you are forced to sleep in, and spending extended periods of time on social media or watching TV. The bottom line is if you are doing something to escape or cope with whatever stressors you are dealing with, you will slowly interrupt your progress.

Without connection to others, you will be forced to live in your head. Yes, you will be subject to your thoughts and reactions. Over time you may find yourself in quite the habit of spoiling one of your most natural healing abilities, and that is the experience of your raw emotions. Think of this habit (i.e., disconnection) like squirting lemon into milk. You have spoiled and soured something nourishing—your raw emotions. As such, you will begin to feel drained rather than energized by what you are feeling.

Jocelyn had lost her husband after twenty years of marriage. To help herself cope with the loss, she kept herself busy. Although being around other people seemed to help lift her spirits, she had a difficult time being alone. When she was alone, the feelings she had been working hard to keep at bay surfaced. Since she had worked so hard at avoiding them, she would often get overwhelmed and begin to wonder if something was wrong with her. She would then criticize her feelings, telling herself that she should be in a better place by now.

Self-criticism and judgment are some primary ways people disconnect from feeling. These behaviors (reactions) keep you feeling trapped in old dynamics (ways of communicating with others). Another way you may disconnect from feeling is by rushing, which is described in the following section.

RUSHING

If I were to ask you when are the times of your day that you are most impatient, you would be likely to tell me it is when you are in a hurry. Rushing is one of the easiest ways you can negatively interfere with the processing of your emotions. Not because you want to get from one place to another but because rushing interrupts, controls, or alters the way something is happening. Let me explain.

> I once had a client call me in a state of emergency. He said, "I don't feel well, and I am going away. Can you do a quantum healing session on me?" I suggested he wait until he returned from his trip so that we didn't rush the process. He got upset with me and decided to go to another healer. You cannot rush healing. If I feel scattered or busy, I will not take on a client. This is because I am not feeling the energy—and the healing, my friend, comes from feeling not reacting.

We are often most impatient when we ourselves are feeling overextended or are in a moment of transition. When it comes to detoxing your emotions, it is important to notice how you may inhibit the process, not just for yourself but others. This will be discussed more in the final chapter, where I focus on how to help others through an emotional detox. For now, consider keeping this in mind: when people are in transition, they typically are not breathing. This is when we are most likely to resort to quick fixes. You can use the steps of the detox to slow down and tune in.

MISUSING FREE WILL

Think of free will as your freedom of choice. Just as it is your free will to choose a detox smoothie over a hamburger, you also have a choice whether to process or overprocess your emotions. Come from a place of fear and you are likely to overprocess; give yourself a chance to come from love (by incorporating the C.L.E.A.N.S.E. steps into your life) and you will benefit from your whole emotions.

Most of us have been trained to select what emotions we tune in to according to how good they make us feel. If something makes you feel good (like getting flowers or a compliment), then you will allow yourself to indulge, but if it doesn't, you learn to push it away. Fear is not the problem; it is your reaction to fear that leads to toxicity and self-sabotage. The detox shows you how this is counterproductive— that once you truly process your emotions, all energy becomes good and beneficial.

During the emotional detox, you can choose to eliminate your reactivity to fear. If you choose to hang on to reaction, that is your free will. I have had to stress this with some clients. I have taken them through the steps and coached them to a place where they can feel their raw emotions; they experience the benefits but then turn right around and use their free will to dissemble their emotional flow.

It is as if they are choosing to remove the process from their life. They want a quick fix or they become afraid of their own power (manifesting). The challenge is that quick fixes cause you to lose energy, which will lead to increasing reactivity (thinking). No worries—the steps will dissemble these tendencies when practiced regularly over time.

ATTACHMENT TO PAIN

When you attach yourself to pain, you are committing to a practice of suffering. This makes your emotional detox seem messy and like hard work. Emotions are not work; they are an experience. It's often said, "Suffering is the degree of resistance we have toward pain." Your emotions are one of the most natural things about you. When you avoid experiencing your pain, you are creating man-made fear, meaning it is something you created unnaturally.

You know you are attaching to pain if you are busy labeling your experience. This way of handling resistance inflates the stories in your head. It isn't until you pay attention to and honor your emotions in the absence of resistance that this will begin to change. I must admit this was a challenge for me. It wasn't until I was able to admit how I was self-sabotaging by reacting to my emotions (rather than experiencing the wholeness of them) that I would be able to move forward (without hesitation) in my marriage. Instead of reacting, I chose to focus on new ways to enhance the process and allowed the steps to detox old ways, helping me to manifest a new way of being.

ENGINEERING THE MOMENT

One of the subtler ways we self-sabotage the processing of our emotions is by engineering the moment. Rather than experience your whole emotions, you might tamper with your environment so that what is in front of you becomes a closer match to how you feel inside. Let me explain.

Imagine you are in a bad mood and the people you are with are laughing and having fun. There may be a disconnect between how you are feeling and the way they feel. Rather than feel your feelings, you might tinker with the energy in the group so it feels more in line with your inner experience. You might say something negative or bring up an uncomfortable topic.

These types of subdued disturbances are unconscious ways we have learned to deal with discomfort. The challenge is that this way of coping depletes energy and will train the body to hold reactivity (toxins). As you learn to digest your whole emotions, there will be moments of discomfort. The discomfort is not the problem; how you handle it is.

Engineering the moment is one of the ways marketing can be so successful. For example, advertisers get us to believe diet soda is somehow a better choice than regular. They match what you are feeling inside (energetically) by demeaning the other choice. You might not feel better drinking diet soda; it is simply a closer match to the quality of your energy. Someone who chooses diet is trying to control (resist) his calorie (energy) intake. This is a brilliant approach to reaching consumers' subconscious minds.

I realize now how much I used to engineer the moment in my marriage. I had a difficult time when my husband was feeling frustrated. To distract myself from my feelings, I might join in his frustration to make us both feel better. I might agree our lawn was too much work and that the chores never seemed to get done. Today I handle this differently.

Here are some other ways you might engineer the moment:

- Changing your tone of voice (e.g., making it sound like you are fine when you are not)
- Trying to fix people's pain to deal with your own
- Wanting things to always be better
- Distracting yourself from your feelings (e.g., pretending you have an important message on your phone)
- Redirecting the focus off you and onto someone else (e.g., talking about your kids)

IMAGINARY HITS

Imaginary hits are false attempts at gaining energy. Like taking a shot of espresso, an imaginary hit may give you a quick boost; however, it loses its kick over a short period of time. When it comes to your emotions, it is important to pay attention to ways you might give yourself a temporary lift as opposed to feeling your emotions. Quick fixes such as people-pleasing, approval seeking, and gossip may give you a rush of adrenalin, yet because they don't allow you to process your raw emotions, once again the energy won't last.

This is because underneath imaginary hits is an unconscious desire to want things (you) to be (feel) better. Imaginary hits are ways you might try to prove rather than feel your worth. This makes you think and work harder. Living life in this way undermines the energy of your emotions.

Susan was great at taking on projects. She enjoyed the challenge, and when they were completed this gave her a sense of satisfaction. This seemed to last for a little while—until she could find another project to sink into. Once Susan learned the steps of the detox, the energy from her actions and efforts started to last longer. Rather than focus on the result, she would period- ically tune in to her emotions (via the seven steps) along the way. Going about her tasks in this way gave her the same feel- ing of completion she had at the end; only rather than waiting until it was over, she realized she could cultivate that experience (through the processing of her emotions) throughout the entire project.

It would be through the steps of the detox that I too would learn this. Once you rinse reactivity from the body, you'll find only one emotion: *love*.

ABSORBING ENERGY

One of the most frequent ways people sabotage the processing of their emotions is by taking on (absorbing) the energy of other people's emotions as if they were their own. They have learned to empathize by carrying the load. Rather than listen and be present to others, they allow themselves to become energetically immersed in their pain. What they don't realize is they are not carrying the emotions of others but rather the reactivity (toxins). You know if you are absorbing another person's emotions when you leave a con- versation or situation feeling upset, rattled, distracted, or powerless. This can create symptoms such as trouble sleeping, distractibility, and anxiety.

Like a sponge that is heavily soiled, soaking up other people's reactivity can make you feel sluggish and less effective at detoxing (cleaning) your bodily functions. This makes processing your emo- tions seem like an impossible, overwhelming task. Whole emotions become buried, and as a result you get accustomed to living in a fear- based reality. You know this is happening because you feel stuck. Although you may have a strong desire to make changes, help, or make a difference, the burden of carrying people's reactivity makes these things difficult to do.

The next chapter provides you with insight on how to set healthy, conscious energetic boundaries. This is important particularly for people who are in the human services, education, and healthcare professions, such as nurses, healers, teachers, and mental health practitioners. It is also critical for parents and caregivers.

LOYALTY TO LOW ENERGY

Another way you may sabotage the processing of your emotions is through loyalty to low energy. Just as you might stay loyal to your hairdresser (even if you are not always happy with your haircuts), you can also stay loyal to low energy. One of the most frequent ways this happens is through worrying. Yes, if you are a worrier, then you are truly committed to low energy.

Many of us have been trained to see worrying as a form of love. This gives you the false impression that your love is reliable. You might believe that when you worry, you are being consistent support for another. The challenge is that worrying obstructs your ability to process your emotions, increasing the likelihood that you will overthink and agonize over what has happened (past) or what could happen (future). Since the processing of your emotions can happen only in the present moment, this way of helping others never gives you any inner movement. Therefore, the toxins (reactivity) are held in place. This makes life seem like you never get a break. There is always something to deal with. It is only when you truly allow yourself to process your whole emotions that these dynamics and coping mechanisms will begin to change.

TAXING ONESELF

When you tax yourself, meaning you take on too much without receiving much in return, this can block your ability to process your emotions. Here is the thing: when you overextend yourself, perhaps by taking on extra responsibilities without setting limits, your body has no choice but to take a back seat. Instead you rely on your brain to get you through the day and to remember, sort out, and perform necessary tasks. This separates your mind (brain) from your body. In order to process your emotions well, it is essential that they are united. Otherwise, you are likely to pump out extraordinary amounts of energy, which can lead to strain, physical exhaustion, and tension.

Tim had a tendency to tax himself by feeling bad for others. He might choose to stay home rather than do something fun because he felt bad that his mother would be alone. The story he told himself was that he did not want her to feel lonely. As I coached Tim through the steps, we would discover through Step 2 (Look Inward) that he was holding onto old feelings of being excluded in grade school. He could recall several occasions when he felt lonely. Because he never allowed himself the chance to fully process and gain energy from this emotion (reactivity), it was still interfering with his life. The reality is that his mother wanted him to go out and have fun. She felt burdened by his tendency to withdraw himself socially. It would be through these types of awarenesses and getting past this way of holding on (overprocessing) that his emotions would change.

If you are a fast talker or find yourself driving white-knuckled down the highway, you may be avoiding the processing of your emotions. You must be mindful, my friend, because you run the risk of being taken advantage of. Employers, parent-teacher associations, and other people/groups with tasks to assign love people like you. As you give yourself time and space to process your emotions, this will naturally change. It is not to say you won't still pitch in now and then; however, you will be able to do it with less guilt (*Hallelujah!*) and worry over what other people are going to think.

CLEANSING TIP: TAMING TRANSITIONS

One of the best things you can do during a transition (when reactivity is higher) is take a moment to stretch. Stretching your arms over your head or tilting your head from side to side (e.g., right ear to right shoulder, left ear to left shoulder) is a way to process your emotions. Stretching helps to release pressure from your connective tissue, where unresolved emotions tend to nest themselves. Notice how taking a stretch shifts your breathing, allowing you to take a deeper inhale and longer exhale.

CHAPTER 7
HOW EMOTIONAL DETOXES ARE ENHANCED

"The standard of success in life is not the money or the stuff—the standard of success is absolutely the amount of joy you feel."

—Abraham-Hicks Publications

Emotional detoxes are enhanced by increasing access to emotions. We've focused on how emotions are obstructed; next we will pay attention to ways to become more open to them. This openness is what makes the difference between *doing* the steps and *embracing* the process. It is key to manifesting. The more you embody the process—truly feel your emotions—the more energy you will gain. What you choose to focus on—love, happiness, freedom—will be propelled by the energy of your whole emotions, rather than held back by states of reactivity.

Once my levels of reactivity went from high to low, I could go beyond the surface of my emotions. This allowed me to dig deeper, and that is when I discovered the tools you are about to learn. Authenticity, connection, having choices, humility, opening your heart, being interested, and staying in your lane all enhance the process, helping you to manifest the life of your dreams.

AUTHENTICITY

I do my best not to lie, and if I do, you are likely to see it written all over my face. Before the detox I considered myself an authentic person, living my life according to the values and morals I talk about and teach. However, being your authentic self involves more than morals and ethics. It is also learning how to genuinely feel your feelings rather than match them according to what is happening around you.

If you learned, like me, to adjust your behavior and actions according to the way other people see you or how you would like them to see you, then you are denying the authenticity of your feelings. According to author Mel Schwartz, LCSW, "Most of us are too concerned with what others think of us. As such, we may disguise or manipulate features of our personality to better assure that others aren't judgmental or adversely reactive to us. If I worry about what others think of me, then I manipulate my personality and communication, either to seek approval or avoid disapproval."

For me, personally, the feelings I had only scratched the surface of what I was truly experiencing. When I accessed emotions, rather than staying stuck in one way of thinking, heavier and deeper feelings began to surface.

I have never been a big fan of red roses. Particularly when they are put together with baby's breath, they remind me of a funeral. My husband never knew this about me because I didn't want to hurt his feelings. Looking back, I now find it apropos that the day I found out about the affair, there were a dozen red roses sitting on my kitchen table. Perhaps this was a foreshadowing of how hiding my true feelings would finally be put to rest.

I have been to my fair share of funerals, and they make me feel so uncomfortable. I never quite know what to say and how to act. Smile, be glum, put your head down, look up—it can all be so overwhelming. I also cry at the drop of hat, and this can be so embarrassing in a large crowd. I often wonder if the way I feel about red roses relates to how I never processed my emotions around these types of things. Instead I clutched the nervous energy closely like a handbag.

Since red roses happened to show up in the beginning of my detox journey, I felt they were symbolically connected to my healing. In many ways, they stood for the fear of loss and unresolved grief I was carrying. I was right—the way I felt about red roses did not represent my true feelings. It was a reaction to my inner experience. This shifted the way I saw red roses. Rather than remind me of funerals, I understood them as being tied to the trigger of unexpressed grief (denial, sadness, shock, fear, anger).

It is through authenticity you will be able to reach some of your core emotions—ones that you may have been burying for quite a while. One way to increase your authenticity is to stop trying to be perfect. If you are criticizing others (or in my case red roses), then, darling, you might be looking for things to be delivered or mended in a perfect way. See imperfection as a sign that you have an open mind. People who embrace imperfection have a way of turning garbage into fine art. By being open, I could learn the difference between being authentic and reacting. To enhance the detox formula, it will be important for you to check in with yourself now and then and ask, "Are these my authentic feelings or am I having a reaction?" Trust me, there is always more. This chart helps make clear the differences between reactions and authentic feelings.

REACTING	BEING AUTHENTIC
Critical, fearful	Open, vulnerable
Adjusting yourself to gain approval	Tuning in to your inner movement
Avoiding conflict	Choosing connection
Limiting accessibility	Allowing transparency

During my healing journey, I adjusted myself (e.g., tone of voice) when I asked my husband to take care of something for me. When he responded in a negative tone, I thought (just like a child tattling), *Wait till I tell the therapist about this one.* What I didn't realize at the time is that this tit-for-tat thing was me pushing away my authenticity. I adjusted my tone so he wouldn't disapprove of my request, not because I genuinely was feeling the energy.

I am not a fan of the phrase "Fake it until you make it." When it came to my marriage, I was faking it too often but holding back and adjusting my true feelings to keep the peace. This is no longer the case. You can fake it all you want, but in general people (particularly those you are closest to) can sniff you out. They know you are not being you, so how can you expect them to relax and trust your intentions? More than this, how will you ever know how to trust yourself?

Being authentic means letting your guard down, opening up to going deeper, and allowing truth to surface and transparency to come through. The more authentic you are, the more self-esteem you will gain. The steps will support this development. Let me tell you, if you have made it this far already in the book, you are already beginning to connect to your whole emotions. This is so exciting! It is happening. Now let's continue.

CONNECTION

My mother called me during my emotional detox to say she was upset about her breakup with a long-term boyfriend. She started the conversation with, "Sheri, he abandoned me *again*."

"Mom," I said, "don't you see? It is the same dynamic you had with your mother? One minute she wanted you there, the next minute she was shooing you out the door. It is all connected to the past; nothing is separate." Then I gave her the first four steps of the C.L.E.A.N.S.E. process.

Mom later texted, "Sheri, this morning's conversation helped me so much. You are so wise, thank you." I was used to this role with my mother, and I also knew I had inherited some of her trauma. Part of increasing the accessibility to your emotions is to acknowledge and surrender to how everything is connected. When you solidify your beliefs and experiences to timelines, you block this entryway. The steps are designed according to the spiritual laws of connection, which function off timelessness. This is in your favor, because it will be through timelessness that you will be able to digest, complete, and receive the energy of your stored emotions, even the ones that have been passed on through your family line.

If you are like me, you have worked hard to be different than your parents. You may have learned from their mistakes and told yourself you will do it differently. I am here to tell you to relax. You are not the same person, and your spiritual purpose has its own unique blueprint. However, when you deny your inherent connection to others, you suppress your emotional flow.

It is normal and healthy for relationships to move in and out of states of connection. It is when you stay in disconnection, however, that resistance begins to seep in, and along with that comes a deep suppression of your emotions. It is during moments of disconnection that I encourage you to go beyond what is being presented. What is happening may be linked to your past or might be a twinge of fear for your future. Relax and soften these timelines. True states of connection can happen only by experiencing the now. Sure, rejection and betrayal can feel awful; however, when you disconnect yourself from your emotional flow, you are deceiving yourself. Rather than blame yourself or others, see these moments of disconnection as opportunities to cross timelines and release deep-seated emotions. Take a breath (inhale, exhale), and let's move on.

CHOICES

Here is what I know: emotional pain is inevitable, and the level of pain you experience is a choice. Yes, when it comes to the duration, frequency, and intensity of emotional pain, you always have a choice. Resistance (fear) keeps pain alive like nothing else. Kick and scream through process, and more is likely to come. Emotional detoxes are enhanced by your ability to be clear and open to your choices. If you want people to shut down their emotions, then make them feel like they have no choices in the matter, and like a toddler having a tantrum, you will see them put up a good amount of resistance. On the other hand, when you can pause, listen, and notice your choices, your body will release. Sure, you may get a little nervous from having to make decisions. However, it would be far worse if you didn't have any choices at all.

Your body naturally loosens when you know you have options. This is because the energy of choice is connected to your free will. It is inherent in the natural flow of your life force. Your soul was never meant to be demanded, controlled, confronted, or coerced; these are all forms of reactivity. If you are not sure what your choices are or you are too afraid to make decisions, the steps will help you purify this uncertainty or fear. Until then, however, it is important to honor and strengthen your connection with choice. Notice how you get to choose when to connect to your soul. Each time you breathe, pause, close your eyes, and smell the air, you are strengthening this connection.

HUMILITY

Spiritual teachers like Mother Teresa remind us to serve. Having a "how will I serve?" rather than a "what will I do?" mindset allows us to feel and connect to what we are manifesting without attachment. When we are in service, we are sharing our feelings. However, helping without awareness, as a reaction rather than an act coming from compassion, can wear you down over time, depleting the precious energy needed to propel what you are creating.

> If you have made a terrible mistake in your life—perhaps you have had an affair or betrayed someone you love—know with humility you can and will heal the situation. Focus on serving, and all will be well.

Having humility strengthens your ability to listen, take responsibility for your part, and be open to new ideas. As you practice and display these behaviors, you will find you not only put yourself at ease but also those around you. It is your sense of ease that allows you to embrace your emotions with open arms. Here are some ways your body may respond differently (energetically) to helping versus serving:

HELPING	SERVING
May be dominated by one person	On the same playing field
Can feel like "doing"	Is feeling
May bring on stress	Eases stress
Focuses on the problem	Focuses on solution and partnerships
Can lead to a few people burdened	Builds community

OPEN HEART

We cannot get to joy with a closed heart. Our heart is the gateway to emotions, and it is through this emotional flow that we manifest. You may already be familiar with how your heart opens when you go out in nature, listen to music, or give someone a hug. The challenge is learning how you keep an open heart even amid hardship.

I have found we misuse—and in some cases *abuse*—our hearts. You may deal with negative people or stress by shutting down. You know this because you might get tense in your face, tight in your shoulders, and a gripping sensation around your chest area. These are signs of resistance.

Many people are unsure how to handle these stressors. Rather than set clear boundaries or digest the emotions that are being triggered, they hide behind their emotional barricade and clam up or lash out. No matter how much you tell them to set limits, say no, or stop paying attention, they can be reluctant to set boundaries because they subconsciously believe these will cut them off from love. They have learned with love you tough it out, take it "like a man," or hope for the best. This could not be further from the truth. Strengthening boundaries focuses energy for manifesting. Otherwise, attention is likely to vacillate. You may find yourself moving from fear to joy. Think of boundaries as focusing a lens on what you are creating. In my case, I chose to focus on resiliency rather than resistance.

BEING INTERESTED

Your interests support your manifesting potential. I can't tell you how many clients share with me how much they have a desire to pursue unexplored interests. Your interests are so important because they connect you to feeling. When you don't allow yourself to feel, this is what can lead to behaviors such as overeating or drinking. You may have an interest in writing, astronomy, or photography—no matter what it is, allow yourself to explore. This will enhance your C.L.E.A.N.S.E. practice. *Go for it!*

After about a year into my C.L.E.A.N.S.E., I started to feel my dreams. This is different from thinking about them or wanting them to come true. I genuinely began to feel like I was living what I had always hoped for. Many things were the same—my home, my family, my car—however, the way I felt was different. As a result, seeds I planted years ago were beginning to sprout and thrive.

As my interest in helping others increased, my clients began saying things in sessions like "I am so angry" and "I want to tell everyone to fuck off."

"I get it," I'd say. Then I would tap into my raw emotions. Closing my eyes, I'd hover my hands over the crown of my client's head, feel everything, and listen for guidance. The results were amazing! This happened repeatedly. The triggers were gone, and clients told me they felt so much lighter. Am I a superhero? No, I was more interested in *feeling* a solution than *finding* one.

I am sure you have tried many things and may even be skeptical right now. Be open, curious, and interested, and you will access the strength, wisdom, and healing power of your whole emotions. Imagine walking into a new gourmet restaurant—the aroma and ambience would make you interested in the menu. This is the feeling I'm referring to. Let go of the need to know what is next and instead be *interested*. You might be pleasantly surprised.

STAYING IN YOUR LANE

If you were driving in your car and were distracted by what was happening on the other side of the road, you might accidentally swerve into another lane. This could put you and someone else at risk for getting hurt. When it comes to accessing your emotions, you will also benefit from developing the practice of staying in your lane, being mindful not to swerve into other people's emotions.

A wonderful therapist and friend named Ana Zick introduced me to the phrase *staying in your lane*, and it helped me stay. Each time I began to meddle or get tangled in things that didn't involve me, I would say to myself, "Stay in your lane." As you are choosing to become aware of and value your emotions, it is important that you take yourself out of the hot seat, give yourself a break from having to take on other people's stuff—their emotions and ways of interacting. Instead, let people handle themselves in their own ways, even if it isn't *your* way.

> When you swerve into other people's emotional lanes, you may be picking up their reactivity. This is one of the ways we interrupt our ability to manifest. We will support others better by digesting our whole emotions.

Learning to listen and honor the pain of others while staying in your lane reflects how you are on the way to creating joy. One way to get there is to look to outside supports. Not just therapy but other activities that will encourage you to process your emotions—things like singing, photography, physical fitness, or social groups.

You see, when you put yourself in the middle, you are in a damned if you do, damned if you don't position. You will never win. If you are nervous about setting clear boundaries, the Emit step will support you. For now, I want you to notice how you might jump in and rescue others. This is how it looks:

BEING IN THE MIDDLE (NONACCESSIBLE)	STAYING IN YOUR LANE (ACCESSIBLE)
Managing other people's emotions	Tuning in to your sensations (Step 2)
Fixing other people's problems	Encouraging others to be direct
Texting about others	Taking a break from group messages and chats
Directing others (e.g., talking for them)	Allowing others to speak for themselves
Having an "I'll do it" attitude	Asking for and accepting help
Reporting for someone else	Staying out of it

CLEANSING TIP: DOWNLOADING JOY

Picture an item to which you feel a connection. It may be a necklace you love, a special coffee mug or blanket, your bike, prayer beads, or a crystal. While sitting quietly, close your eyes and visualize this object. Imagine you are touching it, and say aloud, "May you bring me joy." Let your emotions flow through you. Like a computer downloading data, you are downloading joy through the flow of your emotions from your associations with the object. This is a manifesting visualization—the beginning of learning how incredibly powerful you are.

CHAPTER 8
THE EMOTIONAL DETOX WARRIOR

"Anyone can find the dirt in someone. Be the one that finds the gold."

—an interpretation of Proverbs 11:27

Emotional detoxes help us to become warriors but not in the way you might think. Right now, you may picture warriors with great big swords, fighting off evil and destruction. As you move through the C.L.E.A.N.S.E. formula, you will begin to see it differently. I know I have. Before the detox I had taken many risks in my life but not like this one. This detox was by far one of my most courageous journeys. This is because it isn't just a matter of facing fear but also having the nerve to follow the sensations all the way through to joy.

Being a warrior has nothing to do with power or control. It is your ability to weather out the storm, trusting that it is Mother Nature's way of getting you to rebuild again. My hope is you will turn to unity. That you will use it as an opportunity to simplify your life, focus on what truly matters, and become closer to your most natural state: joy.

The new warrior is not hard, forceful, or demeaning. It is soft, subtle, gradual, respectful, and intentional. It embodies a deep sense of courage and trust that you already have everything you need. Remember: no one has the power to take joy from you. No one—not your mother, father, teacher, priest, friend, boyfriend, boss, mistress, husband, neighbor, no one. This is because joy is an internal experience that penetrates to your soul.

THE C.L.E.A.N.S.E. WAY: YOUR DAILY PRACTICE

Following is a rundown of elements of C.L.E.A.N.S.E. you can incorporate into your daily routines.

CLEAR

You have four choices:

1. Finger press to tone the vagus nerve

2. Fear tap

3. Cat and cow or other type of stretch

4. Rubbing the palms of your hands and placing them on your forehead

LOOK INWARD

Ask yourself: *How do I feel in my body right now?* (Refrain from direct answers; feel sensation.)

EMIT

Redirect your awareness to the present moment and put boundaries in place.

Inhale, and on exhale utter a sound such as "hum," pressing in your navel and lifting your pelvic floor.

ACTIVATE JOY

Expand your heart and third eye (on inhale) and send your energy outward like a laser beam as you connect to joy.

NOURISH

What I appreciate about _____ is_____. (Don't forget to include yourself.)

SURRENDER

Offer your joy and emotional flow to Mother Earth for healing.

EASE

Build trust by talking about your feelings rather than reporting your fears and thoughts. Notice if you are breathing from your chest. If so, go through the formula a second time.

BEING A CLEANSER

A cleanser is someone who commits to a practice of embracing whole emotions through the C.L.E.A.N.S.E. formula. I am so looking forward to hearing how much better you are going to feel, as well as how much the formula has transformed your life. For you, I also look forward to the ways you will connect to joy.

It took a while for one of our daughters to call her father "Dad" again. Unfortunately, the way it worked out for us, the older girls knew more than we would have liked. I hadn't noticed she hadn't been calling him "Dad," but my husband did. "She called me it twice today," he said. "What?" I replied. "'Dad.' She called me 'Dad' two times," he reiterated. It would be moments such as these when we would stumble upon pure joy.

In many ways, my daughters were going through their own version of an emotional detox. Through the process of watching my husband and me, they began to learn to feel safe, connected, and worthy again. Whether or not someone is using the C.L.E.A.N.S.E. formula, there are ways you can support friends and family members through challenging times.

SUPPORTING SOMEONE THROUGH AN EMOTIONAL DETOX

Without awareness, supporting others through an emotional detox can take its toll, making the supporting partner or loved one feel hopeless, rejected, and frustrated with the process. This reaction supports rather than dissolves the vicious cycles that may have led to the detox in the first place. I have supported countless families as they have helped loved ones through the symptoms of anxiety and depression. I always tell them that the main thing they can do to support their loved ones through the process is to listen without judgment. I realize this is no easy task.

One thing that makes it so difficult is how much you already know about the person who is going through the detox. You may have known this person for a while, observed—and even experienced—his habits and pitfalls. It is important that each day is treated with a fresh start. What happened yesterday stays there. The moment you go to the past, you are interrupting the potential an emotional detox offers. Stick with the formula instead, and keep in mind these suggestions:

- Listen, listen, and listen more.
- Let them know you understand what they say or feel may change; you just want to give them a private, confidential place to talk.
- Ask them what they need.
- Send a card not a text.
- Speak softly and watch your abruptness.
- Invite them out to dinner.
- Praise and give tons of hugs.

If you are the one going through the detox and you are feeling unsupported by family and friends, this means you are going to have to be clearer about what you need. Be mindful of your expectations. Watch to see if you take note about how you are being supported (or not) and how others might do it "better." Also, watch yourself to see if you are projecting on or mind reading others. Ask yourself if you are experiencing (feeling) your discomfort or projecting (e.g., lashing out, assuming, or predicting) your fears onto others. For example, I needed to be clear with my husband that I needed reassurance, that saying he was sorry could never feel old to me. With that communicated, I had to be okay if his way of reassurance was sitting next to me and being present. He was learning to allow me to experience my feelings (through the detox) without needing to fix or make things better. Just because you say you need reassurance doesn't mean you get to control the way it happens.

The bottom line is that detoxing, when handled with compassion and respect, is a gift to both you and your loved ones. They are the gateway to deeper, intimate, and trustworthy relationships. If you are feeling rattled or uncomfortable in the process, this means you too can benefit from a detox. Take note that feeling rattled or uncomfortable is different from being abused (verbally, mentally, or physically); if this is the case, all bets are off. Safety and health are the priority before any detox can be put into motion.

ORGANIC LIVING

When it comes to an emotional detox, the C.L.E.A.N.S.E. formula supports organic living—agreeing to a life of whole emotions. Rather than see conflict as a problem, organic living means you view things as a *reaction*. Then, just as you might rinse pesticides off your berries before eating them, you make a decision to decrease your levels of reactivity, digesting your whole emotions before engaging with others.

> I once had a client who was having a terrible fight with her sister. Each of them was highly reactive (defensive). I said to her, "I know what you think about your sister. Close your eyes, take a deep breath, and tell me what you feel. The moment you allow yourself to heal this relationship, you will have everything you want and desire—you'll be living organically. The choice is yours."

Organic living is about healing and nourishing your relationships, accepting the bumps and bruises along the way as opportunities (rather than reminders) to deepen your connection to joy.

As reactivity dissipates and emotional flow increases, organic partnerships are made possible. Organic partnerships are based on a *confidence in connection*. Once you are connected to your whole emotions, you realize how reactivity contributes to turmoil. It is your belief in connection that heals. As a result, you begin to take things less personally. It is through your organic partnerships you will naturally release old wounds, mistakes, and mishaps, as they will be rinsed through your body. The following chart highlights what this may look like.

OVERPROCESSED PARTNERSHIPS	ORGANIC PARTNERSHIPS
Project fears and anxieties onto each other	Deactivate reactivity before speaking to each other
Rush conversations	Set aside a private time to talk
Notice each other's faults or weaknesses	Notice and state what each other appreciates
Focus on individual needs first	Set the intention to notice the good in each other
View emotions as threats	View emotions as opportunities
Focus on protecting	Focus on healing

SHARING YOURSELF

I once asked my husband jokingly, "Do you know which coffee mug is my favorite?" He took a few guesses and then I shared with him, "It is the sage-colored one I got at the pottery shop." A little over a year later, standing in the kitchen where I first learned about the affair, I found my favorite mug next to a fresh pot of coffee. Only this time, there was a note there as well: *Good morning. I love you.*

Joy is simple and fresh with raw emotion. Yet it is one of the most durable and reliable frequencies you will ever reach. With joy, you will be able to withstand any storm and come out in better shape than you were before. Joy will keep you focused. A detox warrior knows this. With that said, choose joy today by sharing yourself. Trust. Be vulnerable. You have the tools, and remember love always wins!

CLEANSING TIP: DAILY REFLECTION

Take a moment now to think of someone you admire. This could be a friend, stranger, celebrity, athlete, poet, sibling, etc. What is it about that person that makes you look up to her? What qualities in her do you feel are praiseworthy? You wouldn't admire those qualities if you did not have them yourself. Somewhere inside of you these qualities and characteristics exist. If you admire someone for her patience, somewhere in you is patience. The same goes for what draws you to a book, program, or class. You wouldn't be attracted if you didn't have the ability to receive what it holds.

As I leave you with this final cleansing tip, know you have everything it takes—otherwise, you would never have picked up this book in the first place. You are ready! If you would like to further your detox experience, go to my website (SheriannaBoyle.com), where I will be posting classes; yoga C.L.E.A.N.S.E. videos; and C.L.E.A.N.S.E. labs, workshops, and retreats.

AFTERWORD: BEING YOURSELF

Breath by breath, joy is pulsating through you right now—clearing what you don't need while pulsing what you do. To live a life of joy means noticing what comes naturally. This means choosing the path of least resistance. With that said, don't assume this path is without challenge. Otherwise, how else will you discover some of your greatest attributes, one being your ability to love? I leave you with this final thought from Dr. Wayne Dyer: "Remember that your natural state is joy. You are a product of joy and love; it's natural for you to experience these feelings. You've come to believe that feeling bad, anxious, or even depressed is natural....Remind yourself as frequently as necessary: *I come from peace and joy. I must stay in harmony with that from which I came in order to fulfill my dreams and desires."*

Until we meet again.

Naturally yours,
Sherianna

ADDITIONAL RESOURCES TO INCREASE EMOTIONAL FLOW

ALTERNATE NOSTRIL BREATHING TECHNIQUE

I highly recommend this technique! It helps you deepen your breath and reach the depth of your lungs. Begin by sitting up tall either crossed-legged on the floor or in a chair. Gently press your shoulders back and down. Place your chin parallel to the earth. Soften your eyes. Take your thumb on your right hand and close off your right nostril so that you are exclusively breathing out of your left nostril. Breathing from your lower abdomen, begin to inhale slowly (inflating the sides of your waist) to the count of one, two, three. Pause at the top of the inhale for one count, then exhale out of the same nostril, pulling in your navel to the count of one, two, three, four. (Your exhale is one count longer than your inhale.) Pause. Then using your right hand again, close off your left nostril using your ring finger. Repeat the same count on this side. Do this for three to four rounds, and notice how relaxed and open you become.

TURMERIC

Turmeric is a spice that comes from the turmeric plant. It has high anti-inflammatory properties. Besides finding it in the spice aisle, you can also find it in the form of a supplement. It is used as a natural medicine for conditions such as headaches, arthritis, fibromyalgia, itchy skin, and more. Turmeric, to me, is an essential yet affordable way to support your detox. I often put it on my salads, and I take one capsule a day.

HEATING PAD

By placing warmth on your abdomen or heart, you can help calm down and soften the resistance of your emotions. I love to use aromatherapy heating pads. Most can be heated in the microwave. At ShopBodySense.com, you can find a variety of heating pads for your neck, feet, and hands, as well as eye pillows.

CRYSTALS

Crystals can be a conduit for healing. Those who have studied their properties find they can be useful for increasing the flow of energy in your body as well as within your environment. They can ward off negativity while promoting relaxation. Some crystals come as small stones that you can place on your desk or windowsill. You can also wear them as jewelry or put them in your pockets. If I know I am entering a heavy or possible toxic situation (e.g., a heated meeting or bar room), I might be inclined to put some crystals around my neck. A few essential crystals are selenite (for clearing negativity), rose quartz (the crystal of unconditional love), and kyanite (for decreasing our resistance).

CRYSTAL ELIXIRS

Crystal elixirs (made by infusing water with the healing energies of crystals) are a form of medicine that can help move people through emotions and stuck patterns. Stones are here on Earth to help us let go of our addictions: addictions to behavior patterns, emotions, substances, or even TV. They work deeply and permanently in our subconscious level of being and have the capacity to move energy on many levels, even upgrade our DNA. Turtle Sun Healing, a holistic healing arts organization run by Ali Zick Pack, provides personalized crystal elixirs for clients. You can learn more at www.turtlesunhealing.com.

SOUND THERAPY

Sound therapy is a form of vibrational medicine. It is often used through instruments such as tuning forks, singing bowls, gongs, etc. You can find sound therapy in wellness and healing centers. Personally, I prefer crystals bowls. When my husband and I were healing, we attended a few crystal bowl circles together. We both found it relaxing to lie on yoga mats next to each other, holding hands as the vibration penetrated our bodies.

GET A NEW PILLOW

Changing your pillow can give you a surprisingly fresh start. When you sleep, you release the stress from the day. Your pillow and bed are two of the places you discharge all this negative energy. I once had a client who got rid of her entire mattress after getting a divorce. She couldn't bear to sleep in the old energy.

COLONICS

Colon hydrotherapy helps put your digestive system back into balance by naturally cleansing toxins. You can find a certified colon hydrotherapist by going to the website of the National Board for Colon HydroTherapy at www.nbcht.org.

SQUAT STOOL

Squat stools are used on the toilet. They allow you to put your knees above your hips, making it easier to eliminate waste. If you are constipated or suffer from irritable bowels or depression, this may be of interest to you. Since so many of our emotions are digested in our gut, it is important to foster healthy and regular elimination.

SOOTHING TEAS

Herbal noncaffeinated teas such as elderberry, peppermint (to ease digestion), ginger, turmeric, and saffron can help ease tension and create emotional balance.

AROMATHERAPY

Using essential oils in a diffuser or on your skin can help you relax and feel more balanced. So long as the oils are nonsynthetic (organic), using scents is one of the quickest ways to activate the calming centers of your brain. Certain scents have been proven to calm organs such as your heart and liver, as well as your intestinal tract. Lavender is known for its soothing properties, while the scent of sandalwood can help you get grounded. Companies such as doTERRA and Young Living are two reputable sources for finding essential oils online.

MASSAGE/ACUPRESSURE/REFLEXOLOGY

Each of these modalities has its own way of moving your emotions. If you do seek out massage or reflexology, be sure the practitioner is board certified. Also, you want to feel comfortable with your practitioner. This allows you to relax your muscles. If you find you are chatting during a massage about anxieties, this may not serve you as much. Cleansing the body of toxic reactivity requires you to release not engage your jaw muscles.

HEALING MUSIC

Music in general can be healing. I enjoy Steven Halpern's *Music for Healing Mind, Body, and Spirit*, available on iTunes. In addition, the song "Weightless" by Marconi Union has been scientifically demonstrated to promote relaxation—in a study conducted by neuroscientists, it was found to reduce anxiety in participants by 65 percent.

BIBLIOGRAPHY

American Psychological Association. "Our Emotional Brains: Both Sides Process the Language of Feelings, with the Left Side Labeling the 'What' and the Right Side Processing the 'How.'" January 12, 2003. www.apa.org/news/press/releases/2003/01/emotional-brains.aspx.

Brown, Brené, PhD. *Daring Greatly*. New York: Avery, 2012. p. 121.

Carpenter, Siri, PhD. "That Gut Feeling." *Monitor on Psychology*. September 2012. www.apa.org/monitor/2012/09/gut-feeling.aspx.

Chopra, Deepak. "Deepak Chopra's 7-Step Exercise to Release Emotional Turbulence." www.gaiam.com/blogs/discover/deepak-chopras-7-step-exercise-to-release-emotional-turbulence/.

Dinse, Hubert R., Jan-Christoph Kattenstroth, Melanie Lenz, Martin Tegenthoff, Oliver T. Wolf. "The Stress Hormone Cortisol Blocks Perceptual Learning in Humans." *Psychoneuroendocrinology*. March 2017. pp. 63–67.

Dispenza, Joe. *You Are the Placebo*. Carlsbad, California: Hay House, 2014. pp. 76, 178.

Emoto, Masaru. *The Hidden Messages in Water.* New York: Atria Books, 2005.

Hadhazy, Adam. "Think Twice: How the Gut's 'Second Brain' Influences Mood and Well-Being." *Scientific American.* February 12, 2010. www.scientificamerican.com/article/gut-second-brain/.

Hanh, Thich Nhat. *The Art of Communicating.* New York: HarperOne, 2014.

Henriques, Gregg, PhD. "Understanding Emotions and How to Process Them." *Psychology Today.* January 28, 2017. www.psychologytoday.com/blog/theory-knowledge/201701/ understanding-emotions-and-how-process-them.

Koniver, Laura, MD. "The Healthiest Ways to Release Any Stuck Emotions." November 11, 2013. www.intuition-physician.com/the-healthiest-ways-to-release-any-stuck-emotions/.

Levine, Peter A., PhD. *In an UnSpoken Voice: How the Body Releases Trauma and Restores Goodness.* North Berkeley, California: Atlantic Books, 2010. p. 8.

McDermott, Pam. www.capecodcolonics.com.

Pert, Candace, PhD. "Where Do You Store Your Emotions?" http://candacepert.com/where-do-you-store-your-emotions/.

Rodriguez, Tori. "Negative Emotions Are Key to Well-Being." *Scientific American.* May 1, 2013. www.scientificamerican.com/ article/negative-emotions-key-well-being/.

Schwartz, Mel, LCSW. "Seeking Authenticity." *Psychology Today.* August 2, 2012. www.psychologytoday.com/blog/shift-mind/201208/ seeking-authenticity.

Seltzer, Leon F., PhD. "The Path to Unconditional Self-Acceptance." *Psychology Today.* September 10, 2008. www.psychologytoday .com/blog/evolution-the-self/200809/the-path-unconditional-self- acceptance.

Snyder, Kimberly, CN. *The Beauty Detox Foods.* Ontario, Canada: Harlequin, 2013. pp. 61, 62.

Townsley, Cheryl. "Resetting the Vagus Nerve." www.youtube.com/ watch?v=EnCjuPqowts.

van der Kolk, Bessel, MD. *The Body Keeps the Score: Brain, Mind, and Body in the Healing of Trauma.* New York: Penguin, 2014. pp. 33, 81.

Williamson, Marianne. "Marianne Williamson on Recognizing Miracles in Your Life." *The Course of Miracles.* www.supersoul.tv/ tag/marianne-williamson/page/2.

Wolynn, Mark. *It Didn't Start with You: How Inherited Family Trauma Shapes Who We Are and How to End the Cycle.* New York: Penguin, 2016. pp. 22, 60.

INDEX

C.L.E.A.N.S.E. Lab™
www.cleanselab.net

Author and wellness expert Sherianna Boyle's personalized C.L.E.A.N.S.E. LAB™ offers readers the opportunity to work one-on-one with Boyle— and experience firsthand the spiritual freedom and joy a true *Emotional Detox* can bring.

Book your session today at
www.cleanselab.net
